I0866326

THE THAI KITCHEN OF BOO RAAN

SHARING RECIPES FROM DOKKOON KAPUEAK

Lannoo

KOON

I was born in Ubon Ratchathani, a city in the north-east of Thailand near the border with Laos and Cambodia. My family lived in the countryside, where we – just like most people living there – grew herbs and vegetables around the house and cultivated rice on a rented patch of land. At the weekends, I accompanied my father to the paddy field. He ploughed the land with our water buffalo while I caught tiny frogs, which we then brought back home with us to prepare for dinner. My brother Ting and I also used to go fishing in that rice paddy. Father put together fishing rods made from bamboo sticks, nylon wire and a hook, to which we would attach long, fat worms. In the morning, Ting and I would plant the rods in the field and, in the evenings, we would return to collect our catch. Sometimes there were two or three fish, sometimes ten, but somehow, there was always enough fish for everyone. We had a few ducks wandering around in our yard, and they provided us with eggs. The chickens were only butchered on special occasions. Ting and I loved mangos, which we found in abundance near the temples where many mango trees grew. We were allowed to pick up the fruits lying around on the ground, but it was strictly forbidden to pluck a mango from the trees. The adults warned us: if you pluck a mango, one of the spirits from the temple will come after you. Because we were children, you can imagine we didn't dare to disobey. Ting and I did have enough courage to occasionally pick fruit that grew alongside the road. While one of us stood and kept watch for passers-by, the other quickly grabbed something from the tree. Then, as fast as our legs would carry us, we ran off with our loot. In fact, we grew or caught everything ourselves, and the only ingredients we bought were sugar, fish sauce, soy sauce, and oil or lard.

The cooking took place outside, under a lean-to, over clay ovens called *tao* that we covered with a metal sheet. When we had money, we used charcoal; otherwise, we used wood. The children – especially the daughters – were expected to help with the household chores. In the morning, I prepared the fire and started cooking the rice. Sometimes I made omelettes for breakfast. On other days, we ate leftovers from the previous day. Then my brother and I would head off to school, but we returned home at lunchtime to eat. In the evenings, we had another hot meal. Thais don't really distinguish between different mealtimes. Rice with an omelette or soup for breakfast, cold leftovers for lunch and a warm meal for dinner... all those dishes could be served any time during the day. It was a simple life without any luxuries, but we were never hungry. Nature provided us with what we needed.

When I was about ten years old, my parents left for Bangkok to work in the construction industry, and my grandmother came to live with us. Grandma was very *boo raan* – Thai for traditional. She raised me, Ting, and our cousin Tawa with strict discipline. At the weekends, I had to visit the Buddhist nuns to learn about traditional values and customs. In the summer, Ting and Tawa were sent away to the monks for a month. This meant that I had to get up extra early in the morning to cook for them. The food they received was also far more delicious than what we usually ate, but I wasn't allowed a single bite or taste. I can laugh about it now, but at the time, I thought that was extremely unfair.

Grandma taught me everything I needed to know as a Thai woman. She taught me how to be modest, obedient, and humble – values that are very important in Thai culture but which aren't always understood in the West. That included iron discipline, and she taught me what hard work was. As a child, I couldn't always appreciate this strict upbringing, but with hindsight, I consider it a blessing. She gave me the necessary discipline and strength to keep going, even during the more difficult moments in my life.

When I was 16, I travelled to Bangkok to find work there. My niece took me in, and I found a job as a dishwasher in a fish restaurant. I was exposed to a whole new world of flavours. At the restaurant, I tasted things such as mussels, lobster, and shrimp for the first time. Moreover, Bangkok is a metropolis where you can taste food from all parts of the world. I distinctly remember my first hot dog, bought at a local 7-Eleven, an American convenience store. I couldn't believe what I was tasting! That soft bun, the sausage, the combination of mayonnaise and ketchup, the white onion, the pickle... This was so delicious! Just like pizza baguettes, another one of my favourites. But *farang*, or Western food, was generally too expensive. I usually cooked in my apartment for myself and my friends.

One day, the chef at the restaurant showed me his collection of spice mixtures, curry pastes and other flavourings. To his amazement, I could tell him which ingredients each pot and jar contained, often just by smelling them. From that moment onwards, I was occasionally allowed to help in the kitchen, and I started learning the tricks of the trade. Sadly, the restaurant closed its doors soon after that, and I had to look for other work. After a short training, I ended up in one of the many sewing workshops just outside Bangkok, where I spent two years sewing sports and golf bags. When I'd had enough of sewing bags, I did a hairdressing course and returned to the heart of Bangkok to start work as a hairdresser. The idea of setting up a noodle stand at a market one day was always at the back of my mind, but to do that, I needed money, which I didn't have.

When my aunt, who was married to a Belgian, invited me to come to Knokke, I had no intention of staying there. But life is full of unexpected turns. In Knokke, I ran into Patrick, a businessman and foodie with a passion for Thai cuisine. I started to work for him at events, and before I knew it, we had opened a restaurant together in 2016. The rest is history.

PATRICK

I'm a businessman in the events sector, but I'm also very passionate about cooking. I'd always been incredibly interested in Thai cuisine for some reason, even though I'd never been to Thailand before. The flavours fascinated me, and I wanted to learn more. Everywhere I went, I hunted for Thai restaurants where I could try new things.

In 2013, I ran into Koon in Knokke. When she told me that she could cook Thai food, I asked her to prepare something for an American friend who was coming to visit. Walter was a huge fan of Thai cuisine as well, and he would often tell me about the many Thai restaurants in Miami. Koon made *laab kai,* chicken satay, Thai beef and *pad Thai* for us, dishes that all went down incredibly well. That gave me an idea. I knew that Koon was looking for a new challenge, so I asked her whether she'd be interested in cooking at events. Event catering is often very traditional, and I thought it would be interesting to put something more exotic on the menu. They were often simple dishes such as noodle soup, Thai beef, or chicken satay with fresh peanut sauce, but they were a tremendous success. During golf tournaments, we would stand at the ninth hole with a stand and serve a small, but authentic, Thai tasting menu. People were so enthusiastic that they invited us to come and cook for guests at their homes. One client led to another, and Koon and I started developing a small network. Koon cooked, and I assisted her. Our only goal was to serve people delicious food; we hadn't even begun to think about setting up a restaurant.

After two years of working together, I felt it was time to make this arrangement a bit more stable. We didn't yet know how we were going to do it, but I was thinking of something to do with catering and events that fitted in with my work.

Meanwhile, I'd bought a house on Edward Verheyestraat, a street in Knokke, from a postman who was about to retire, and I wanted to renovate it. I didn't have a specific use in mind yet, but I kept coming back to the idea that I could turn the ground floor into a restaurant where Koon could cook. I wanted an open-plan kitchen, so guests could see their meals being prepared. It soon became clear that we also needed the second floor so people could sit comfortably to eat the food. I convinced Koon by assuring her that we would start out small and simply see where things would go. Koon and I had experience cooking for large groups, but running a restaurant is a whole different kettle of fish. If things didn't work out, it wasn't the end of the world. I could always sell the renovated house.

The restaurant opened its doors on 25 November 2016. We chose the name Boo Raan because we wanted to serve our guests only traditional Thai dishes without any additional flavourings. The ingredients came from Thailand and were prepared just the way Koon had learned at home. We chose to adopt a sharing menu; multiple small dishes would be served for the guests to share according to traditional Thai custom.

Boo Raan

The second surprise came eight months after the opening when Gault&Millau gave us the Best Asian Chef of the Year award. Thankfully, we had found people to help us by that time. Nit and Noot assist Koon in the kitchen, Draw takes care of the *mise en place,* and Nina comes to help us at the weekends. They are all Thai women who come from the same region as Koon.

In 2021, none of us saw the Michelin star coming. And, although it was a great compliment to be awarded such a famous prize, not much has changed for us.
We continue to cook as we have always done. In the future, we would like to focus on growing our own Thai herbs and look for wines that go well with Thai food.
In that respect, we want to stay *boo raan* and would prefer to choose organic wines made by small producers – wines that are fruity, mellow, and just as authentic as the dishes we serve.

Finally, the idea of writing this book was around before we even started the restaurant. From the very beginning, people kept asking us how they could make certain dishes. With this book, we would like to show everyone how they can cook delicious Thai food, as long as they use the best ingredients and prepare them properly.

On the day of the opening, culinary journalist Bruno Vanspauwen came to eat with us. He wrote a glowing article about the restaurant and gave us the highest possible rating: four plates. Thanks to that article, we were inundated with reservations, and we had to open the second floor. Because we didn't have any staff at this stage, we had to do everything ourselves, with only a dishwasher to help us. We were overwhelmed by the success. During those first months, we literally worked night and day.

MICHELIN

CONTENTS

Superstar

Maggi

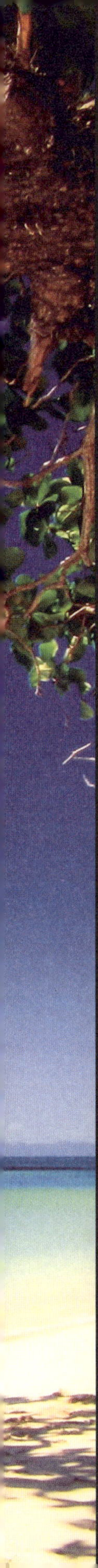

THE LAND OF SMILES

Thailand is one of the most popular holiday destinations in Asia. That's not surprising, considering there is something for everyone. Thailand has cities bursting with life, historical sites with temples and palaces – many of them UNESCO World Heritage sites – breath-taking nature, and tropical islands with white, sandy beaches and crystal-clear waters. Not to mention the unsurpassed cuisine, where every imaginable flavour is perfectly combined. It's no wonder that Thailand is also known as 'The Land of Smiles'.

GOOD TO KNOW

Name
— Kingdom of Thailand

Location
— South-East Asia

Capital city
— Bangkok

Total area
— 513,120 km^2 (+ 3219 km coastline)

Climate
— tropical

Population
— 69 million

Language
— Thai

Religion
— Buddhism (94.6%)

Currency
— baht (1 euro = 37 THB / 1 GBP = 44 THB) (*August 2021*)

Airports
— Bangkok, Phuket, Chiang Mai

The central region and the 'City of Angels'

Thailand's central region consists of a large green plain through which the Chao Phraya River runs. Prosperous communities once settled in this fertile region, which today is home to the capital city, Bangkok, known in Thai as *Krung Thep*, or the 'City of Angels'.

Bangkok is a fascinating combination of traditional and modern. In the old part of the city, you can get lost in the traditional neighbourhoods and marvel at stunning palaces and temples and Bangkok's rich heritage. The city's business district is packed with skyscrapers, but you can also spend hours shopping in the hypermodern shopping malls or go for drinks at one of the many trendy rooftop bars. Foodies will find themselves in culinary heaven among the hundreds of street-food stands scattered around the entire city, or they can enjoy a gourmet meal in one of the world-class restaurants.

Visitors looking to learn more about the country's history can visit Ayutthaya, just a two-hour drive from Bangkok. This was the capital of the Siamese kingdom from the 14th to the 18th century. The ruins are a UNESCO World Heritage site and take you back to medieval Thailand.

Would you like to learn more about the ingredients involved in Thai cuisine? Then Samut Songkhram, or the 'Land of the Floating Markets', is a must. Local farmers travel to this market every weekend on flat-bottomed boats laden with homegrown vegetables, fruits and hand-crafted products. This colourful floating market is a feast for both the eyes and the senses.

Finally, Kanchanaburi is worth mentioning; here you can see fantastic waterfalls and spend the night in a floating bungalow.

The north, with its rolling hills and majestic temples

In Thailand's northern region, you will find tall mountains, dense forests and many rivers running through deep valleys. Here, the Lan Na Kingdom – which literally means 'Kingdom of a Million Rice Fields' – was founded in the 13th century. Chiang Mai is the region's largest city. It owes its name, 'Rose of the North', to its many temples with their characteristic golden spires, layered roofs and impressive wood carvings. Rice fields and tea plantations surround the city. You can also visit elephant sanctuaries or go on adventurous trekking journeys through the jungle. The northernmost province is Chiang Rai. Chiang Rai is situated in the legendary Golden Triangle region and has a lively border trading market. Hidden among the mountains, you will find Mae Hong Son with its stunning natural surroundings and colourful people. Sukhothai is a must for amateur archaeologists. This was the first capital city of Siam in the 13th century and is considered the cradle of Thai civilisation and culture. The Sukhothai Historical Park – the ruins of the ancient city – is a UNESCO World Heritage site and is particularly known for its annual Festival of Lights, which takes place on the eve of the full moon in November. As soon as the sun

The south, with its paradise-like islands and crystal-clear seas

The south of Thailand is mainly a peninsula that separates the Gulf of Thailand in the east from the Andaman Sea in the west. The mainland, with its forests and plantations, is abundantly green. On the coast, you'll find the most beautiful tropical beaches, and the islands are truly idyllic for holidaymakers. These include the well-known island of Phuket – the 'Pearl of the Andaman Sea' – or the province of Phang Nga with its breath-taking bay that achieved cinematic fame in the James Bond film *The Man with the Golden Gun*. Krabi is a wonder of nature with its white sandy beaches and staggeringly tall cliffs that plunge down into the blue-green waters. The islands of Phi Phi, Lanta, Jum and Ngai are idyllic spots for hedonists, as are Samui, Phangan, Tao and Mu Ko Ang Thong on the east coast. It won't surprise you that this region is heaven on earth for scuba divers.

Authentic Thailand in the north-east

The north-east of Thailand is a rugged plateau called *Isaan* by the Thai people. It's a thinly populated area with little tourism where farmers grow jasmine rice. Nakhon Ratchasima, or *Korat*, is an idyllic combination of wild nature and civilisation. Khao Yai National Park is a UNESCO World Heritage site known for its impressive biodiversity. Here you can go on fantastic treks past gorgeous waterfalls and panoramic views. Or you can soak up the local culture during a visit to Phimai temple, an 11th-century Khmer sandstone monument. Chef Koon was born in Ubon Ratchathani. This is also home of the Pha Taem National Park, with its savanna full of enchanting waterfalls and sites where you can admire mysterious prehistoric paintings. The stunning landscape is shaped by the mighty Mekong River. Near the source of this river lies the town of Loei, where people wake before the crack of dawn to give alms to the Buddhist monks before going off to work in the fields. Udon Thani is home to the more than 5,000-year-old archaeological site, Ban Chiang. Romantics can go on a boat journey on Red Lotus Lake over waters that stretch for miles.

** For more information, visit the Thailand Tourist Authority website https://www.tourismthailand.org/home or send an email to info@tourismethai.fr.*

The islands on the east coast

The east coast is just a few hours' drive from Bangkok, but it's a region overlooked by many visitors. That is unfortunate because it's an area bursting with orchards filled with unusual types of fruit and is an absolute must for fish and seafood lovers. The Chonburi province is known for its beaches, Bang Saen and Pattaya. People looking for peace and quiet visit Rayong with its beautiful coastline or the magical tropical beaches on islands such as Samet, Man Nok and Talu.
In Chanthaburi, you can get acquainted with the traditional Thai way of life in the lively neighbourhoods surrounding the country's largest Catholic church, situated on the banks of the Chanthaboon River. You will also find unique markets here that sell gemstones as well as many other items. The furthest province, Trat, is home to a few pristine islands such as Chang, Mak, Rang, Kood and Kham, with powdery soft sandy beaches and wonderfully balmy waters.

In each part of Thailand, you can taste the country's soul in its traditional dishes. Thai cuisine is exceptionally delicious and full of flavour; it's a perfect reflection of the qualities of this unique country and everything it has to offer. Thailand is the ideal destination for anyone who wants to get further acquainted with Asia – whether it's through a family vacation, an adventurous trek through the jungle, a relaxing beach holiday, a thrilling diving adventure, or a culinary journey of discovery.

THE THAI KITCHEN

Thai cuisine is one of South-East Asia's most refined cuisines. Thai chefs are constantly searching for the right balance between sweet, sour, savoury, spicy and bitter. Each region has its own typical dishes and flavours, but there are also clear influences from India, China, Laos, Burma, and Malaysia. This results in a very rich, diverse cuisine that is nonetheless characterised by its light, fresh flavours. Ingredients such as fish sauce, shrimp paste, chilli peppers or galanga root are hardly subtle, yet Thai cooks know how to combine them into perfectly balanced flavours that stir all the senses.

Rice is the main ingredient of any Thai meal. All the other dishes are simply flavourings to go with the rice. Everything is served in small bowls and plates, after which the host or hostess says 'Kin khao' – which literally translates to 'eat rice' – to indicate that you can start the meal. Most dishes are not eaten with chopsticks but with a fork and spoon.

THE MOST IMPORTANT INGREDIENTS

RICE & NOODLES

A meal isn't complete until the rice has been served. Jasmine rice is the most commonly used rice in Thailand, and it's prepared with a special technique (page 34). The term 'jasmine' refers to both the scent and the structure of the rice.

Thais also use white and black sticky rice, to be served with *laab*, for example, or eaten as a dessert. The precise instructions for making sticky rice are given on page 34.

In addition, Thais like to eat noodles. *Sen lek* are fine rice noodles; *sen yai* are thick, flat noodles. Then there's also *kai chab,* flat noodle sheets sliced into squares that curl up into small tubes when you cook them. All these noodles are made from rice flour. We also know *bamee,* egg noodles, and *ka nom jeem* (Thai spaghetti, page 96), made from fermented rice noodles.

VEGETABLES

Besides rice, a lot of fruits and vegetables are grown in Thailand. Some of these are not as well known in the West.

Unripe papayas are the main ingredient of green papaya salad, or *som tam*. They taste deliciously fresh with just a hint of spice. The ripe version of this fruit is eaten by Thais as a dessert.

Thai aubergines are nothing like the aubergines you find here. They differ in shape, colour and flavour. There are three varieties: light-green round balls the size of a plum, green pea-sized balls, and elongated light-green aubergines that are slightly bitter and are therefore excellent for the digestion. You don't have to peel them, and they are used whole or cut into pieces in all sorts of dishes.

Thais use mostly shiitake mushrooms instead of more common types of mushrooms. The caps are prepared, while the tougher stalks are used to make broth.

Thai green asparagus is very thin and soft, so you don't have to peel it. Thai spring onions are also thinner and have a more subtle flavour than their Western counterparts.

The typical celery from Thailand is smaller than the celery sold here, and it also has a more refreshing taste. Thai shallots are small and have a pink hue, and tend to be on the sweet side, just like Thai garlic.

Long beans, also known in English as 'asparagus beans' or 'snake beans', are long pods that have a flavour similar to that of green beans but more intense.

There are around 1,500 types of bamboo, of which about a hundred species are edible. Of these edible varieties, only a dozen or so are commonly used in the kitchen. Fresh, young bamboo tends to be more bitter and must be boiled twice for a long time before you can eat it. Bamboo shoots are the offshoots of a young bamboo plant. You don't usually find fresh shoots here, but you can buy them in vacuum-sealed packages or glass jars. They have a subtle flavour and contain plenty of vitamins and minerals, with little fat and practically no sugar.

FRUIT

Thais eat fruit primarily as a dessert. Some types of unripe fruit – such as mango or papaya – are also used in savoury and spicy salads.

Some other types of fruit are not well known in the West, such as rose apple, guava, pitaya or dragon fruit, *mangosteen*, *longan* (a type of lychee), *rambutan*, jackfruit or *nangka*, durian, *sapodilla* and pomelo. When you buy them at the market in Thailand, they often come with a dip made from salt, sugar and chilli peppers. Green mangoes are eaten as a snack with a sweet and spicy dip containing fish sauce.

สับปะรดภูแล
แพ็คละ 60 บ.

CHILLI PEPPERS

Thai cuisine can be quite spicy for Westerners, but you can always dial down the spice in a given dish. Simply removing the seeds and the membrane makes chilli peppers less spicy. The *bird's eye chilli,* in particular, is spicier than the chilli peppers you find in shops here.

Chilli peppers are called *phrik* in Thailand. They were brought into the country by the Portuguese in the seventeenth century and became very popular. They add colour and spice to your dish. Dried chilli peppers give the dish a full, mild flavour. Prepare fresh green chillies as quickly as you can to keep their fresh scent and spiciness. They are slightly spicier than the red varieties. The chillies with the most pronounced flavour are the yellow chillies, which are used to full effect when mixed with other spices in a curry paste.

HERBS, SPICES AND OTHER FLAVOURINGS

Thais use a lot of herbs to flavour their food. Coriander is the most commonly used herb – not just the stems and the leaves, but also the roots with their distinct aroma and spicier flavour. The roots are often ground to a fine paste in a mortar with other ingredients such as garlic, salt, or peppercorns. The paste then serves as the foundation of a dish. The leaves and stems are incorporated into soups, salads, fish dishes or curries. If you can't find coriander root, use the stems.

Basil also occupies a permanent spot in the Thai kitchen. The three types of basil Thais use vary from the varieties we used in Europe and America.

Thai basil (*horapa*) is slightly sweet with a hint of aniseed. It's mainly used to add spice and flavour to stir fries and curries. Holy basil has a peppery flavour that is enhanced when you cook it. This type of basil is particularly suitable for heartier dishes. And, finally, lemon basil is the perfect flavouring for soups and fish dishes.

Thai chefs also like to add mint to fish or mince dishes. Its fresh flavour contrasts nicely with the spicy chillies.

Lemongrass and kaffir lime leaves give dishes a fresh, sour, lemony flavour. You can bruise the lemongrass stalk and cook it in its entirety along with the dish, or you can finely chop the softer centre and add it in. Kaffir lime leaves can be added in their entirety or sliced julienne and then added. Or you can grind both the lemongrass and kaffir lime leaves down into a curry paste.

The knobbly peel of the kaffir lime *(citrus hystrix)* is used to flavour dishes. The juice from the kaffir lime is too bitter for consumption. Thais use this juice to rinse their hair.

Galangal root is also known as *laos*, or 'Thai ginger'. It looks like ginger, and the taste slightly resembles ginger, yet it's different. Galangal root is spicier than ginger and gives curry pastes or soup a distinctive aroma.

Fingerroot, known as *grachai* or *krachai*, is a type of elongated ginger root that looks like fingers. You can slice and sauté the root or grate it. The taste is reminiscent of ginger but fresher. The root has a robust and distinctive flavour, so you need to be careful with it. Fingerroot is excellent for digestion, but you shouldn't eat too much of it.

Tamarind, or *ma kham,* gives Thai dishes a sour flavour – like vinegar, but more subtle. The fresh fruit is almost impossible to find here, but you will find pressed tamarind in Asian supermarkets. Soak the paste in warm water for a couple of minutes before kneading. You can sieve the leftover water and use it as tamarind juice later.

Soy Sauce, Fish Sauce, Fermented Shrimp Sauce

Soy sauce is made from fermented soybeans. In Thailand, mostly the lighter variety is used; it's a less viscous and saltier version of dark soy sauce. This type is a natural soy sauce without the addition of roasted wheat.
In addition to soy sauce, fish sauce *(naam pla)* and fermented shrimp paste *(kapee* or *krapi)* are also used to add salt to dishes, giving them their distinctive umami flavour. You can also make a spicy dipping sauce with these ingredients. Thai fermented fish sauce and shrimp paste have a very intense aroma. Keep them tightly sealed when storing them in the refrigerator and use small quantities as a flavouring.

Tofu, Fish, Meat Seafood

Thais get their protein from tofu, fish, seafood, and meat. They generally use far smaller quantities than we do. Moreover, they are prepared so you can easily eat them with a fork or a spoon, or as finger food.

Tofu is made from soybeans. It has a neutral flavour and can be used in stir fries or soups.

Thais also love scampi, shrimp, and squid. Fish is usually prepared whole, often steamed in a banana leaf. Chicken *(kai)*, pork *(moo)* and beef *(neu)* are typically cut up into small pieces, so you can easily eat them with a spoon or a fork.

Palm and Cane Sugar

Palm sugar is made from the sap of the coconut tree. The liquid is reduced to a brown paste. The sugar has a slight caramel flavour and aroma and is less sweet than the granulated sugar used in the West. You can buy it as a paste or in liquid or powder form.

The cane sugar is very similar to the granulated sugar you find in the West, but it has a slightly different flavour due to the molasses added to it. That's why Thai cane sugar is brown.

Coconut

Thais eat almost no dairy products. Instead, they use coconut milk and coconut cream. Coconut cream is made by grating coconut flesh and soaking it in hot water before pressing. Look for a high-quality, creamy variety and try out a few brands. The best coconut milk is not entirely white but has a light-grey colour.

Tapioca

Tapioca flour comes from manioc or cassava root and, among other things, is used to thicken sauces.

THE METHODS

GRILLING

Thais love to grill their food on a small barbecue. They often sit on the ground around the barbecue and place their food straight onto the grill. The charcoal adds to the flavour. More delicate ingredients such as fish are wrapped in a banana, a pandan, or a coconut leaf. The leaf makes sure that the fish doesn't dry out, and it adds flavour. Moreover, the leaves are naturally non-stick.

DEEP-FRYING

Thai fast food is usually deep-fried, but sometimes deep-fried foods are offered as part of a larger meal. These dishes are always accompanied by some greenery or fruit to compensate for the fat. We usually deep-fry in a large wok with two handles. We let the oil get really hot to make the frying process as quick as possible and make sure that no fat gets into the ingredients. We use a slotted spoon to scoop the deep-fried items out of the fat and leave them to drain before serving.

STEAMING

Steaming ensures that the nutrients, aromas and flavours of the dish are preserved. The best way to steam is to use lots of fresh ingredients and stack different steaming pans or baskets on top of each other. The bottom pans contain the ingredients that need to cook the longest; the ingredients that need to be steamed only briefly are stacked on top. You can also use this steaming method to heat up food or keep it warm.

STIR-FRYING

With stir-frying, preparation is key. All the ingredients must be cut into small, bite-size pieces, so you can work fast once you start to fry. The vegetables should be cooked al dente and still have a bit of a crunch. That's how they retain their taste and texture.

Fry the vegetables at as high a heat as possible and work quickly. Shift the cooked ingredients off to the side, so they don't cook any further. Use a wooden spoon to move the ingredients around in the wok.

KITCHEN UTENSILS

WOK

In Thailand, a wok is not only used for stir-frying; it's also used for deep-frying or steaming.

Turn up the heat as high as you can when stir-frying. The bottom of the wok is the hottest part and is used for frying. The sides are slightly less hot; so, any ingredients that are almost cooked are shifted to the side. You use a wooden spoon or spatula to turn and move the ingredients.

If you want to use the wok for steaming, you need a rack that sits halfway down the wok. Pour a layer of water 5 centimetres deep into the wok and bring it to a boil. You can wrap the ingredients to be steamed in a banana, a pandan, or a coconut leaf if you wish. Place the ingredients or leaf-wrapped foods on the rack. Cover the wok with a lid and let the ingredients cook slowly. You can also put a bamboo basket in the wok on top of a cooling rack used for baking.

To deep-fry, heat the oil in the wok to a really high temperature. Remove the deep-fried items with a slotted spoon.

MORTAR AND PESTLE

A mortar and pestle are essential for anyone wishing to prepare Thai food. You will find mortars and pestles in all sizes at kitchenware shops. They're usually made from stone, but there are also wooden ones available. Use the pestle to finely grind the ingredients: nuts, chilli peppers, lime leaves, herbs... Always grind the harder ingredients down before adding the softer ones. Otherwise, you'll have difficulty grinding everything down to a paste. You can also use a blender, but that gives the paste a very different flavour and a less fragrant aroma.

RICE & NOODLES

Rice is a daily staple of the Thai diet. There are many different types of rice out there, but the main difference is between normal (jasmine) rice and sticky rice, which are prepared in different ways. Thai noodles are also made from rice. Making them requires some work, but they are a delicious addition to any stir fry.

RICE

JASMIN RICE

If you have a rice cooker, use that to cook your jasmine rice. Cooking rice without a rice cooker requires a little more work.

For 1 to 2 people

Method 1

Add a cup of rice to a pan with plenty of water. Wash the rice by stirring the rice with your hands and drain off the water. Repeat this a couple of times until the water runs clear. Put the rice in a pan and add two cups of water. The water level should come up to the first knuckle of your finger when you place your fingertip on the rice in the pan.

Bring the water to a boil over high heat. Keep stirring until the water level drops to below the level of the rice, and then lower the heat as much as possible. Put a lid on the pan and let the rice cook for another 5 to 10 minutes.

Method 2

This method is simpler because you don't have to measure the precise amount of water that goes into the pan.

Rinse the rice as described above, but this time, add the clean rice to the pan with plenty of water. Bring to a boil and cook over a high heat, stirring constantly. Drain the water off from the pan and cook the rice covered over low heat for 5 more minutes.

STICKY RICE

Sticky rice is eaten with both savoury dishes and desserts. As the name says, it's sticky, so you can roll it up into a ball and eat it with your fingers.

Put the rice in lukewarm water and leave it to soak for at least an hour to an hour and a half. The longer you soak the rice, the better. You can even soak the rice the night before you need it. Drain off the water and rinse the rice at least twice. Place a muslin cloth in a steamer basket or pan and add the rice. Steam the rice over boiling water. You know the rice is cooked once the grains start to glisten and become translucent.

NOODLES

Noodles are originally a Chinese dish. Thais do eat them, but it's not really a traditional staple. In the 1930s, the Thai government was looking for a way to raise the market value of rice. Through the promotion of rice noodles, noodle manufacturers purchased large quantities of rice, driving the price up. Today, noodles are a part of the Thai food culture. For instance, *phad thai,* or stir-fried noodles, has become Thailand's signature dish.

SEN YAI

These broad rice noodles take some time to make, but they're not difficult to prepare. Homemade noodles are subtle in flavour and deliciously chewy. You can use them in all sorts of Thai dishes such as stir fries.

Ingredients

· 2 cups rice flour
· 2 cups tapioca flour
· 2 cups water
· ½ teaspoon salt
· sunflower oil

Extra kitchen equipment:
· steamer
· flat baking tray
· chopping board
· basting brush

Preparation

Combine the rice flour with the tapioca flour, water and a pinch of salt to make a thin batter.

In a steamer, bring water to a boil. Grease the baking tray and the cutting board, brushing them with oil.

Spoon a thin layer of batter into the baking tray. Place the tray on top of the boiling water in the steamer and cover. Steam covered for about 5 to 7 minutes.

Let the batter cool slightly and then remove the batter sheet with a spatula. Carefully pull the sheet away from the baking tray and lay it flat on the cutting board. Brush some oil over the sheet. Make more sheets and stack them on top of each other. Make sure there's always a layer of oil between the sheets. Cut the sheets into broad strips and pull them apart. Use the fresh noodles in stir fries or noodle soup or fill them.

SINGHA

Dishes with MEAT

KAI SATÉ

Ingredients

Makes 12 skewers

- 500 g chicken breast
  or chicken thighs/drumsticks*
- sunflower oil

For the marinade:

- 50 ml coconut milk
- 1 tablespoon curry powder
- 1 tablespoon soy sauce
- 1 tablespoon cane sugar

Preparation

To make the marinade, combine the coconut milk with the curry powder, soy sauce and cane sugar.

Slice the chicken breasts or the meat from the thighs/drumsticks into long strips. Place the strips in the marinade, stir thoroughly to coat the chicken, and cover with a lid or cling film. Marinate the chicken in the fridge for at least an hour, but preferably overnight.

Thread the chicken strips onto satay skewers. Attach several pieces of chicken to each skewer. Make sure that each skewer has about 40 to 60 grams of meat.

Heat a grill pan and grill the chicken satay in a little sunflower oil until golden brown or grill them on the barbecue.

Serve the chicken satay with cucumber dressing (page 204) and peanut sauce (page 204).

** Chicken thigh meat is generally more tender than breast meat. You can buy chicken thighs or drumsticks from the butcher or poulterer. It doesn't matter if the skin is still attached in places, as it only adds flavour to the chicken.*

Ingredients

Makes 40 rolls

- 160 g cellophane noodles
- 300 g chicken breast
- 300 g carrot
- 300 g leek
- 2 tablespoons sugar
- 1 tablespoon sesame oil
- 120 ml soy sauce
- 1 teaspoon black pepper
- 1 packet (40 sheets) square spring roll wrappers of 15 x 15 cm
- 1 egg white
- oil for frying

Preparation

Soak the cellophane noodles in cold water for 10 minutes. Drain and slice the noodles into 4-8 centimetres pieces.

Slice the chicken breast into strips 4 centimetres long, 1 centimetre wide and half a centimetre thick. Grate the carrot and slice the leek into thin matchsticks (julienne).

Combine the chicken with the carrots, leek, sugar, sesame oil and soy sauce. Season with black pepper.

Place the spring roll wrappers on a work surface with one corner facing you. Spoon 2 tablespoons of filling onto the centre of the sheet. Fold the corner over the filling, fold the sides into the middle, and continue to roll. Seal the roll with a little lightly beaten egg white.

Cover the spring rolls with a clean, damp cloth to prevent them from drying out. Heat the oil to 170 °C and fry the spring rolls until golden brown, 6 to 8 minutes. Serve with sweet and sour dipping sauce (*sod priawan*, page 206).

TIP Freeze the spring rolls overnight before cooking them; the wrapper will tear less easily during frying if you do.

Popia tod — *Spring rolls*

KWITIAO

Ingredients

Serves 3 to 4 people

· 1 carrot
· 50 g pickled radish (Asian supermarket)
· 4 shiitake mushrooms
· 1 onion
· 1 spring onion
· 1 clove garlic
· 4 tablespoons oil
· 300 g pork mince (unseasoned)
· 2 tablespoons thin bamboo shoots
· ½ tablespoon palm sugar
· 2 tablespoons soy sauce
· 5 or 6 fresh noodle sheets (page 35)

Preparation

Finely chop the carrot, radish, shiitake mushrooms, onion, spring onion and garlic.

Heat the oil. Sauté the garlic. Add the pork mince and cook until no longer pink. Add the remaining ingredients and let everything cook. Season to taste with palm sugar and soy sauce.

Fill the fresh noodle sheets with the mince filling.

LUI SUAN

Kwitiao lui suan — *Noodle sheets filled with pork mince and vegetables*

TOM KA KAI

Ingredients

Serves 1 to 2 people

- 2 stalks lemongrass
- 1 normal shallot or 3 Thai shallots
- 1 to 2 small red (Thai) chilli peppers
- 2 coriander roots or 4 coriander stems
- 40 g galangal root
- 250 ml coconut milk
- 200 ml chicken stock
- 4 lime leaves
- 200 g chicken (drumstick and thigh meat)
- 40 g shimeji mushrooms
- 1 teaspoon cane sugar
- 2 tablespoons fish sauce
- 2 tablespoons lime juice
- coriander leaves to garnish

Preparation

Bruise the lemongrass stalks, peeled shallot, and chilli peppers. Clean the coriander roots or stems and the galangal root, then slice and crush them.

Bring the coconut milk to a boil together with the chicken stock. Add the lemongrass, shallot, chilli peppers, coriander roots or stems, galangal root and lime leaves.

Slice the chicken into small pieces and add them to the broth together with the shimeji mushrooms. Cook everything in the broth over a low heat.

Add the cane sugar and the fish sauce. Reduce the broth for 3 minutes over a low heat, stirring occasionally. Add the lime juice. Season to taste, adjusting the sweetness (sugar), sourness (lime) or saltiness (fish sauce).

Garnish with a few coriander leaves.

KAENG

Ingredients

Serves 2 people

For the red curry paste (120 ml):

- 10 dried bird's eye chillies, without seeds
- 4 dried chilli peppers, without seeds
- 1 teaspoon ground coriander
- ½ teaspoon ground cumin
- 1 teaspoon white peppercorns, crushed
- 1 teaspoon salt
- 1 teaspoon galangal root, finely chopped
- 2 teaspoons coriander root, finely chopped
- 1 tablespoon kaffir lime peel, finely chopped
- 4 cloves garlic
- 15 g lemongrass, thinly sliced
- 12 shallots
- 1 teaspoon shrimp paste

For the curry:

- 300 g chicken breast or lean chicken thigh meat
- 3 tablespoons sunflower oil
- 3 tablespoons curry paste
- 560 ml coconut milk
- ½ red pointed sweet pepper
- 30 g bamboo shoots
- 4 Thai aubergines (round green balls the size of a plum)
- 12 to 15 Thai pea aubergines (small green marble-sized aubergines)
- 3 tablespoons fish sauce
- 1 tablespoon cane sugar
- a handful of Thai basil leaves + extra

KAI

Preparation

First, make the red curry paste. Soak the dried peppers in warm water. Drain off the water and finely chop the peppers.

Dry-roast the coriander and cumin 1 minute in a non-stick pan until fragrant. Combine them using a mortar and pestle with the peppercorns and grind down to a fine powder.

Grind the crushed white peppercorns together with the salt to a smooth mixture. Peel and finely chop the garlic and shallots. Add the galangal root, coriander root, kaffir lime peel, garlic, lemongrass and shallots to the mixture. Grind everything down to a fine paste.

Add the shrimp paste and the roasted spices and continue to grind to a smooth paste.

The curry paste will keep for up to two weeks in the refrigerator.

For the curry, slice the chicken breast or chicken thigh meat into thin slices and set aside.

Heat the oil in a large pan. Fry the curry paste until it becomes fragrant and starts to change colour. Pour in the coconut milk and stir. Bring to a boil.

Add the chicken to the pan and cook over low heat for 5 minutes.

Slice the pointed sweet pepper into thin strips. Add the sweet pepper, bamboo shoots and all the aubergines to the curry. Lower the heat and add the fish sauce and cane sugar. Let the mixture cook. Add the Thai basil as soon as the chicken is tender. Stir and cook for 30 more seconds.

Serve in deep dishes and garnish with the extra Thai basil. Serve with jasmine rice.

KOON: ‘My mother would say I was a very curious child. In the evenings, as soon as I heard the grinding song of pestles on mortars from neighbouring houses, I would go out and explore. I was barely four years old, but I would ask all the neighbours if I could have a taste of whatever they were grinding down. I soon realised that the same dish tasted different depending on who made it and was characteristic of the lady of the house.

‘A Thai curry paste is always made from fresh ingredients, giving them their deliciously fresh aroma and flavour. The colour and flavours depend on the chilli peppers and herbs and spices used. Red curry paste contains fresh and dried chilli peppers, giving it a milder flavour. Green curry paste is made from green chilli peppers and herbs and is generally spicier. The spiciest are the yellow curry pastes containing Thai chilli peppers and turmeric.

'To make the paste, Thais grind everything down into a fine paste with a mortar and pestle. The mixture must be well mixed and should stick a little when you fry it. You should not see traces of individual ingredients. You can try using a blender, but the aroma is not the same.

'To make the curry, fry the curry paste in the pan and add coconut milk. The other ingredients are added later.'

KWITIAO
MOO DENG

This delicious, hearty soup is ready in no time.

Ingredients
Serves 2 people

For the soup:
· 350 g lean pork neck
· 2 tablespoons moo dang seasoning mix (Asian supermarket)
· 1 tablespoon unsweetened condensed milk
· 1 teaspoon honey
· 1 carrot
· 1 large onion
· 2 litres water
· 5 to 6 coriander roots or 12 coriander stems
· 5 shiitake mushrooms
· 1 clove
· 1 star anise
· 1 tablespoon cane sugar
· black peppercorns
· salt
· 1 tablespoon soy sauce
· 1 tablespoon sunflower oil
· 200 g noodles
· ½ bunch coriander
· 2 spring onions

For the dumplings:
· 150 g lean pork (fillet or tenderloin)
· 1 tablespoon sesame oil
· 2 tablespoons coriander leaves, finely chopped
· freshly ground black pepper
· salt
· 6 dumpling wrappers (Asian supermarket)

For the garnish:
· cane sugar
· fish sauce
· 1 clove garlic
· sunflower oil
· chilli lime (add finely chopped chilli pepper to the juice of 1 lime)
· 1 small red or green (Thai) chilli pepper
· 1 lime

Preparation

Marinate the meat for half an hour in the moo dang seasoning mix, condensed milk and honey.

Dice the carrots into large pieces and the large onion into four wedges. Bring the water to a boil and add the carrots, onion, coriander roots and shiitake mushrooms. Season with the clove, star anise, cane sugar, peppercorns, a pinch of salt and soy sauce. Let the mixture simmer over low heat.

For the dumplings, mince the meat together with the sesame oil, chopped coriander, freshly ground black pepper and salt.

Lay the dumpling wrappers on a work surface and spoon a half a tablespoonful of the meat mixture on each wrapper. Fold the corners into the middle and press the ends together in the middle. Bring water to a boil and boil the dumplings for a few minutes until cooked. Drain on paper towels.

Grill the marinated pork with a bit of sunflower oil in a grill pan.

Soak the noodles in cold water. Soften the noodles just before serving in a bowl of hot water. How long this takes depends on how thick the noodles are.

Divide the cooked noodles over bowls. Slice the pork and arrange the slices on top of the noodles. Put the dumplings on top and ladle a large spoonful of hot soup (and vegetables!) into the bowl. Garnish with fresh coriander leaves and finely chopped spring onions.

In Thailand, the soup is often seasoned with cane sugar, fish sauce, fried garlic, or marinated chilli peppers. To fry the garlic, thinly slice the peeled cloves and deep-fry until golden brown in a bit of sunflower oil. For the marinated chilli pepper, squeeze a lime and mix the juice with finely chopped chilli peppers.

By playing around with these seasonings, you end up with an entirely different soup every time.

Tip → You can also add a few look chin balls to this soup, if desired (see recipe on page 77).

This delicious hearty soup is ready in no time.

KOON: 'Thai food can be a bit dry. Soup makes everything easier to digest and helps the food go down well. That's why soup is not eaten as a first course but is served on the table together with other dishes.'

KWITIAW KAI

Ingredients
Serves 4 people

· 1 carrot
· 1 large onion
· 1 litre water
· 2 chicken drumsticks
· 1 clove
· 5 to 6 coriander roots
 or 12 coriander stems
· 5 shiitake mushrooms
· 1 star anise
· 1 tablespoon cane sugar
· 12 black peppercorns, bruised
· salt
· 1 tablespoon soy sauce
· 400 g noodles
· ½ bunch coriander
· 2 spring onions

For the garnish:
· cane sugar to taste
· fish sauce to taste
· 1 clove garlic
· sunflower oil
· 1 lime
· 1 to 2 small red or green (Thai) chilli
 peppers, finely chopped

Preparation

Dice the carrots into large pieces. Peel and quarter the onion.

Bring the water to a boil. Add the chicken drumsticks, carrot, onion, clove, coriander roots or stems, shiitake mushrooms, star anise and cane sugar. Season the broth with the bruised black peppercorns, salt, and soy sauce. Cook the chicken in the broth.

Meanwhile, soak the noodles in cold water.

Remove the chicken from the broth and pluck the meat from the bones.

Remove the soaked noodles from the water and briefly submerge them in hot water. Divide the cooked noodles over soup bowls. Add the chicken and spoon a generous ladleful of hot broth over the top. Garnish with the coriander leaves and finely chopped spring onions.

In Thailand, the soup is additionally seasoned to taste with cane sugar, fish sauce, fried garlic or marinated chilli peppers. To fry the garlic, thinly slice the peeled cloves and deep-fry until golden brown in a little sunflower oil. For the marinated chilli pepper, squeeze a lime and mix the juice with finely chopped chilli peppers. By playing around with these seasonings, you end up with an entirely different soup every time.

LAAB

Ingredients

Serves 2 people

- 300 g chicken not too lean, preferably thigh/drumstick meat
- 4 tablespoons water
- 1 tablespoon fish sauce
- 1 shallot
- 2 tablespoons lime juice
- 1 teaspoon roasted chilli powder (page 211)
- 8 sprigs coriander
- 10 sprigs fresh mint
- 2 to 3 tablespoons toasted rice powder (page 211)

Preparation

Chop the chicken very finely with a knife (or have it coarsely minced at the butcher shop). Bring the water to a boil and add the minced chicken. Add 1 teaspoon fish sauce. Let the chicken simmer, stirring, until the chicken is tender. Remove the pan from the heat and remove any excess liquid.

Peel the shallot and chop into thin wedges. Add the shallot, the remaining fish sauce, and the lime juice to the chicken. Season to taste with roasted chilli powder.

Finely chop the coriander and tear the mint leaves into smaller pieces. Stir the rice powder and the herbs into the *laab* just before serving.

Serve the *laab* with sticky rice and crunchy raw vegetables such as iceberg lettuce, cucumber, beans, or endive leaves.

Tip

Don't add the rice powder to the *laab* until the very last minute. Otherwise, the powder will absorb too much liquid, making the dish too dry.

Laab kai — *Chicken mince with lime, shallots, spring onions, coriander and chilli peppers*

KOON: '*Laab* is a typical dish from my native region. It is an *Isaan* preparation, but that's a word I don't like to use much. 'Isaan' literally means "north-east", but it also means "country". Thais from larger cities sometimes use this as a swear word, but to me, it means "pure and simple". It is food that comes straight from nature, home-grown and traditionally prepared.

‘In Thai cuisine, meat is usually cut or minced into small pieces. That’s because we only use a fork and spoon at the dinner table. You won’t have a knife to cut everything into pieces, or the chopsticks used in other Asian cultures. Moreover, it’s much easier to divide dishes up among your guests. Where I grew up, meat was only served on special occasions. By chopping it up into small pieces, we could divide it up to serve more people so that everyone would have a bit of meat.’

KAI
YANG

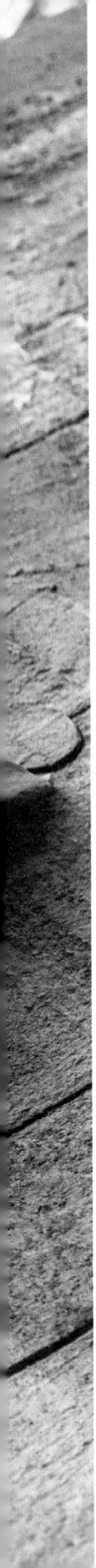

This dish originally comes from the north-eastern part of Thailand, close to the border with Laos. Today, *kai yang* is a countrywide favourite, and you will often find it sold as street food at local market and roadside food stands. The secret to *kai yang* is all about the marinade, to which each chef adds their own twist. Some use ginger or hoisin sauce, but the recipe below is how we make it at Boo Raan.

Traditionally, the chicken is flattened before being slow-roasted. You serve it with white sticky rice, green papaya salad and dipping sauces. These sauces are sweet in the central Thai region and sour in the north-east. Experiment and discover what your favourite *kai yang* tastes like.

Ingredients

Serves 2 people

- 4 tablespoons light soy sauce
- 12 tablespoons coconut milk
- 2 teaspoons palm sugar
- 5 cloves garlic, crushed
- 1 tablespoon black pepper, bruised
- 8 coriander roots or 16 coriander stems
- 1 chicken

Preparation

Combine the soy sauce with the coconut milk and the palm sugar. Add the crushed, peeled garlic cloves and bruised pepper. Finely chop the coriander roots or stems and stir them into the marinade.

Cut the chicken open at the breast, so you can flatten it. Coat the entire chicken with the marinade and leave it to rest in the refrigerator for 2 hours.

Preheat the oven to 220 °C.* Place the chicken on a rack above a baking dish and press the chicken down to flatten it. Bake for 25 minutes in the oven. Spoon some of the juices (and the rest of the marinade) over the chicken. Lower the oven temperature to 180 °C and bake for 20 more minutes.

Stick a satay skewer into the thickest part of the chicken to check whether it's cooked through. If clear liquid seeps out of the chicken when you skewer it, the chicken is cooked.

Remove the chicken from the oven and leave it to rest for 10 minutes under aluminium foil.

* You can also cook the chicken on the barbecue if you wish.

Preparation

Slice the cucumber in half lengthways and remove the seeds with a teaspoon. Slice the flesh into diagonal slices.

Peel the red onion and chop into thin rings. Slice the cherry tomatoes in half.

Combine the cucumber with the peeled red onion, cherry tomatoes and the finely chopped mint and coriander.

Divide the beef into two, 150-gram pieces. Combine the oyster sauce with the soy sauce and freshly ground black pepper. Rub the marinade into the steaks and leave them to rest for at least an hour.

Fry the steaks in a grill pan with a little sunflower oil or on the barbecue. Thinly slice the meat and place the slices on a warm plate. Season with coarse salt.

Combine the cucumber salad with *nam jim seafood* (page 205) and spoon the mixture over the beef slices. Garnish with a little more coriander. Serve with the rest of the *nam jim seafood*.

* At Boo Raan, we use Irish rump steak, but if you like a bit of fat in your meat, you can also use entrecote or ribeye steak. Whatever you choose, make sure the steak is tender.

Ingredients

Serves 2 people

· 1 cucumber
· 1 red onion
· 16 cherry tomatoes
· 50 g mint leaves
· 30 g coriander leaves

For the beef:
· 300 g steak*
· 2 tablespoons oyster sauce
· 2 tablespoons soy sauce
· black pepper
· sunflower oil
· coarse salt

Yam neu — *Thai beef*

These meatballs are pure street food. You can eat them grilled on a stick or in a noodle soup. In Thailand, they're usually bought at the market instead of made at home, but it's not hard to make them.

You can use pork mince, but chicken or beef mince works fine as well. If you decide to use pork mince, make sure it doesn't contain too much fat, but if you use beef mince, use a variety with a higher fat content so the meatballs don't dry out.

The meatballs are made in an unusual way, by squeezing the mince with your fists. Definitely give it a try sometime!

Look

Ingredients

Serves 4 to 6 people

- 400 g pork mince (shoulder cut)
- 1 tablespoon soy sauce
- 1 teaspoon sugar
- 2 tablespoons tapioca flour
- 1 teaspoon baking powder
- 12 black peppercorns
- 1 clove garlic
- 100 g ice cubes

Preparation

Combine the mince in a bowl together with the soy sauce, sugar, tapioca flour and baking powder. Grind the peppercorns into a fine powder with a mortar and pestle and finely chop the peeled garlic. Add the pepper and the garlic to the mince. Mix everything thoroughly in a blender.

Gradually add the ice cubes and continue to blend until the mince becomes sticky. Put the mixture in the fridge to set for 30 minutes.

Put a pot of very hot water on a work surface. Take a handful of mince and make a fist so the mince comes out in an oval shape through the top of your fist. Fold the mince back into your hand and press once more. Dip a spoon in the hot water and scrape the mince from your hand into a round ball.

Drop the ball into the hot water. As soon as the ball starts to float, the meat is cooked. If you don't use boiling water, leave the first balls in the water a bit longer.

Remove the floating balls from the water and set aside to drain.

You can keep the meatballs for up to two days in the refrigerator or freeze them to be used later in a dish.

A Thai barbecue grill looks a bit different from the one you're probably familiar with. The central part is a lid featuring a rounded dome with small slits. The dome slopes down into a circular pan and then the very outer edge goes up at a sharp angle. This lid is placed over a pot holding hot charcoal.

My friends and I eat barbecue made with this almost every week, sitting on the ground around the pot. The circular pan contains simmering broth, and we fry thin slices of meat on the hot lid. It's truly a fantastic dish.

In this recipe, we use pork, but you can also use other types of red meat, chicken, fish, or even shrimp and squid. Choose pork that contains slightly more fat as it will have more flavour. You can also use different cuts of pork together such as pork belly, pork neck and pork tenderloin.

MOO KRATA

Ingredients

Serves 4 people

For the broth:
- 2 litres water
- 8 coriander roots or 24 coriander stems
- 300 g ham hock or pork neck
- 20 peppercorns
- 1 or 2 large white onions
- 2 stalks celery
- splash of soy sauce
- salt

For the barbecue:
- 400 g pork (pork tenderloin or pork neck, with a bit of fat for flavour)
- 25 g sesame seeds
- 5 tablespoons sesame oil
- 4 tablespoons soy sauce
- pepper

Additional ingredients:
- 300 g cellophane noodles
- 200 g pointed cabbage
- 80 g Thai basil

Preparation

Bring the water to a boil and add the coriander roots or stems and the ham hock or pork neck. Grind the peppercorns into a fine powder with a mortar and pestle and slice the peeled onions into wedges. Add them to the broth. Finely chop the celery and add to the broth. Add a splash of soy sauce and a little bit of salt.

Keep the broth warm over low heat and regularly spoon some of the broth into the circular pan surrounding the grill while barbecuing. There should always be liquid in the pan.

Slice the meat into very thin slices. Roast the sesame seeds and combine them with the sesame oil and soy sauce. Season to taste with freshly ground pepper. You can also add an egg to the marinade if you wish. Marinate the meat in the mixture.

Prepare the cellophane noodles according to the packet instructions. Slice the cabbage into 4 x 4-centimetre pieces.

Fry the meat on the barbecue. Put the additional ingredients in the broth.
Eat the meat together with the cooked ingredients from the broth and *nam jum suki* (from a bottle) or *nam jim thua* (page 206). In Thailand, we eat this barbecue with chopsticks.

JIM JUM

Ingredients

Serves 3 to 4 people

For the broth:
· 60 g galangal root
· 2 stalks lemongrass
· 2 small (Thai) chilli peppers
· 1 large tomato
· 3 (Thai) shallots
· 2 litres water
· 300 g beef shin
· 4 lime leaves

For the meat:
· 150 g chicken breast
· 150 g pork tenderloin or lean pork neck
· 150 g sirloin steak

For the accompanying ingredients:
· 300 g pointed cabbage
· 4 spring onions
· 300 g cellophane noodles
· 150 g shimeji mushrooms
· 80 g Thai basil

Preparation

Slice the galangal root. Bruise the lemongrass and chop into large pieces. Slice the chilli peppers lengthways in two, and quarter the tomato. Coarsely chop the peeled shallots.

Bring the water to a boil. Add the beef shin, galangal root, lemongrass, lime leaves, chilli peppers, tomato and shallots. Let the broth steep for a while.

Slice the meat into pieces. Slice the pointed cabbage into 4 x 4-centimetre pieces and the spring onions into not too small pieces. Prepare the cellophane noodles according to the packet instructions.

Cook the meat and the accompanying ingredients in the broth. Serve with *nam jim jeaw* (page 205).

KANOM JEEN KAENG KIEW WHAN KAI

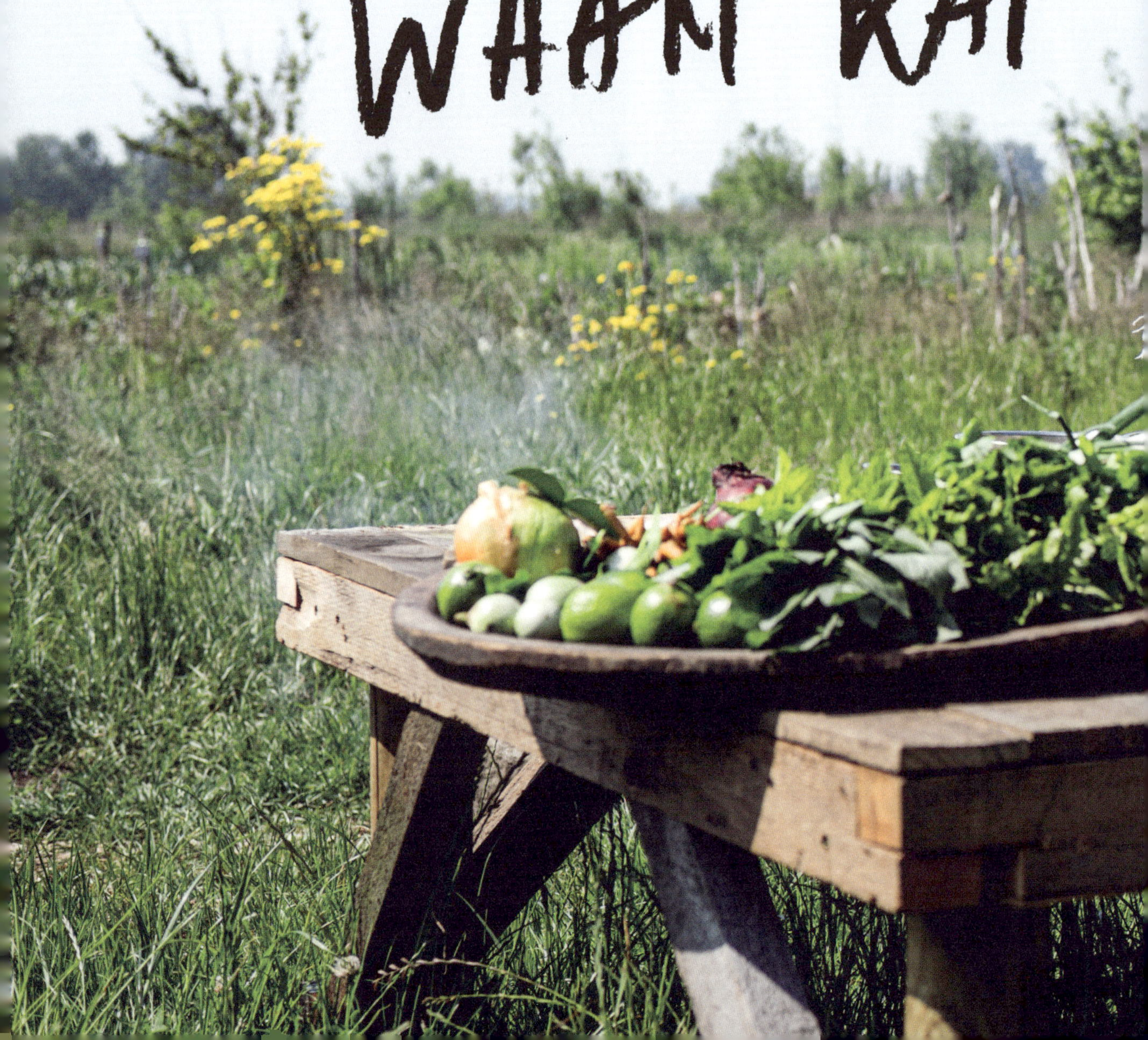

This Thai spaghetti is truly amazing. Instead of the traditional broad rice noodles, you use fermented rice noodles, or *kanom jeen,* which look like spaghetti. These noodles are served with all types of curries and often replace rice in many dishes.

Ingredients

Serves 2 to 3 people

For the green curry paste:
- 1 teaspoon coriander seeds
- ½ teaspoon cumin
- 1 teaspoon white peppercorns
- 1 teaspoon salt
- 10 small green (Thai) chilli peppers
- 1 teaspoon galangal root, finely chopped
- 15 g lemongrass, thinly sliced into rings
- 1 teaspoon coriander root or 2 teaspoons coriander stems, finely chopped
- 1 tablespoon kaffir lime peel, finely chopped
- 3 (Thai) shallots, finely chopped
- 2 cloves garlic
- 20 to 25 g *krachai* (fingerroot - Asian supermarket)
- 1 teaspoon shrimp paste

For the curry:
- 2 chicken breasts
- 3 Thai aubergines (green balls the size of a plum)
- a splash of sunflower oil
- 2 tablespoons green curry paste
- 560 ml creamy coconut milk
- 4 lime leaves
- 50 g bamboo shoots
- 20 Thai pea aubergines (green balls the size of a pea)
- 2 tablespoons fish sauce
- 1 teaspoon cane sugar
- 200 to 280 g *kanoom jeen* (fermented rice noodles)

For the accompaniments:
- 50 g long beans
- 20 g red pointed sweet pepper
- 50 g bean sprouts
- 50 g Thai basil

Preparation

Start with the green curry paste. Combine the coriander seeds, cumin seeds and peppercorns in a non-stick pan and roast them until they start to become fragrant. Grind the spices down with a mortar and pestle, add the salt and set aside.

Chop the chilli peppers into large pieces. Put them in a blender together with the galangal root, lemongrass, coriander root or stems, kaffir lime peel, peeled and chopped shallots, peeled garlic, *krachai* and shrimp paste. Blend well and then add the spices. You can also grind the paste using a mortar and pestle, but that takes a lot of time. A combination of blender and mortar and pestle works best. First, blend all the ingredients in the blender and then continue to grind them down with the mortar and pestle. The curry paste will keep for up to two weeks in a tightly sealed container in the refrigerator.

Slice the chicken breast into strips 6 centimetres long, 3 centimetres wide and half a centimetre thick. Quarter the larger aubergines.

Heat the oil in a pan and sauté the curry paste until it becomes fragrant and starts to change colour. Add the coconut milk and bring to a boil.

Add the chicken strips to the coconut milk and let them simmer for 5 minutes over a low heat. Add the lime leaves, bamboo shoots and all the aubergines. Also add the cane sugar and the fish sauce. Let everything cook over low heat.

Cook the *kanoom jeen* according to the instructions on the packet. Transfer the noodles from the hot water immediately into a bowl with cold water. Take a handful of the noodles out of the water and carefully roll them into a nest shape. Drain on a paper towel.

Chop the long beans into pieces and slice the sweet pepper into thin julienne strips.

Place several noodle 'nests' on a plate, spoon the curry over the top and garnish with the remaining ingredients.

NAM TOK NEU

Ingredients

Serves 2 people

- 250 g sirloin steak
- black pepper
- oyster sauce
- splash of sunflower oil
- 1½ tablespoons fish sauce
- 2 tablespoons lime juice
- 1 to 2 tablespoons toasted rice powder (page 211)
- roasted chilli powder (page 211)
- ½ cup fresh mint, coarsely chopped
- 2 tablespoons lemongrass, very finely chopped
- 2 tablespoons coriander, coarsely chopped
- 2 spring onions, in thin rings
- ½ red onion, peeled and cut into thin rings

Preparation

Marinate the beef an hour in some bruised black peppercorns and the oyster sauce.

Heat the oil and grill the steak to the desired doneness. Remove the meat from the pan, set aside on a warm plate and cover with aluminium foil.

Combine the fish sauce with the lime juice, toasted rice powder, roasted chilli powder (to taste), mint, lemongrass, coriander and onion.

Thinly slice the meat and spoon the fish sauce and lime juice spice mixture over the sliced beef. Serve with sticky rice.

Tip You can also make this dish with pork. The pork version is called *nam tok moo.*

To make *neua yang*, marinate the steak in *saam kleu* (page 211) for at least an hour. Fry the steak in sunflower oil in a grill pan to the desired doneness. Then set the meat aside on a warm plate under aluminium foil for 3 to 5 minutes.

Serve the beef with a bowl of *nam jim jeaw* (page 205) and sticky rice.

The marinade and grilling the meat on charcoal make for an amazingly tender piece of meat bursting with flavour.

Neu yang — *Simple grilled beef*

PANENG NEU

You can make this immensely popular curry with chicken or pork, but we usually make it with beef. It's a milder curry where salt, sweet and Thai basil are the dominant flavours.

Ingredients

Serves 1 to 2 people

For the paneng curry paste:

· 6 large dried red chilli peppers
· 1 teaspoon salt
· ½ teaspoon cumin
· 1 teaspoon coriander root or 2 teaspoons coriander stems, finely chopped
· 1½ teaspoon galangal root, finely chopped
· 1 tablespoon lemongrass, finely chopped
· 3 tablespoons shallots, finely chopped
· 4 tablespoons garlic, finely chopped
· zest of 1 kaffir lime

For the curry:

· 300 g lean beef
· 2 to 3 tablespoons paneng curry paste
· sunflower oil
· 250 ml creamy coconut milk
· 1 tablespoon palm sugar
· 2 tablespoons fish sauce
· 3 lime leaves
· 8 strips red or green sweet or pointed pepper
· 30 Thai pea aubergines (green, pea-sized balls)

Preparation

First, make the curry paste. Soak the dried chilli peppers in warm water. Drain and remove the seeds.

Put the salt and cumin seeds in a mortar or a blender. Grind or finely blend. Add the chilli peppers, coriander roots or stems, galangal root, lemongrass, peeled and finely chopped shallot, peeled and chopped garlic and zest. Grind or blend to a smooth curry paste.

Slice the beef into slices, 4 x 6 centimetres and half a centimetre thick.

Sauté 2 to 3 tablespoons of the curry paste (it should be comfortably spicy) in sunflower oil until it becomes fragrant and starts to change colour. Add the coconut milk and bring to a boil while stirring. Add the beef, sugar and fish sauce. Cook the curry a little longer.

Tear the lime leaves and add them to the curry. Add the bell peppers and the aubergines just before serving.

Preferably you should begin to make this pork satay the day before you want to eat it. The longer the meat is left to marinate, the more tender and juicier it becomes.

Ingredients

Serves 3 to 4 people

- 5 cloves garlic
- 3 coriander roots or 2 tablespoons coriander stems, chopped
- 1 teaspoon black peppercorns
- 3 tablespoons (35 g) palm sugar
- 2 tablespoons oyster sauce
- 3 tablespoons soy sauce
- 1 tablespoon sunflower oil
- 75 ml coconut milk
- 3 tablespoons water
- 500 g lean pork neck
- 3 tablespoons cornflour

In addition: bamboo satay skewers, 5 centimetres long

Preparation

Finely grind the peeled garlic, coriander root or stems and peppercorns in a mortar. Add the palm sugar and continue to crush until the sugar has dissolved. Finally, add the oyster sauce, soy sauce, oil, coconut milk and water.

Cut the pork into slices half a centimetre thick. Add them to the marinade and stir to coat thoroughly. Let the pork marinate in the fridge for at least an hour, but preferably overnight.

Sprinkle the cornflour over the meat and stir to coat. Thread the pork pieces onto bamboo satay sticks and place them on a plate. Leave them to rest in the fridge for a couple of hours.

Fry the pork satay in a grill pan over a high heat or – even better – on the barbecue. Serve with sticky rice and *nam jim jeaw* (page 205).

MOO PING

KERVEL

Dishes with SEAFOOD & FISH

Scampi tempura

Ingredients

Serves 2 people

- 300 g tempura flour
- 75 ml water
- 200 g panko (Japanese breadcrumbs)
- 10 king prawns
- oil for frying

Preparation

Stir 200 grams of the flour with water until it forms a smooth paste.

Put the remaining flour on a plate or in a dish. Put the panko on a third plate or dish.

Remove the heads, shell and devein the prawns. Don't remove the tail. Make 1 or 2 small incisions in the belly, so you can lay them out flat.

Take a prawn by the tail and coat it first with the dry flour, then with the floury paste. Finally, coat the prawn with the panko. Do the same for the other prawns.

Heat the frying oil to 180 °C. Deep-fry the prawns in small batches until golden brown. Drain on paper towels and serve with sweet and sour chilli dipping sauce (*sod priawan*, page 206).

TOM YAM

Ingredients

Serves 2 people

- 2 large tiger prawns with head still attached (8/12 count)
- 400 ml water
- 1 stalk lemongrass
- 35 g galangal root
- 75 g coriander root or coriander stems
- 1 onion
- 1 small red (Thai) chilli pepper
- 5 lime leaves
- 2 tablespoons *nam prik pao* (Thai chilli paste)
- 60 g white shimeji mushrooms
- ½ tablespoon palm or cane sugar
- 2 tablespoons fish sauce
- 3 tablespoons lime juice
- 3 tablespoons unsweetened condensed milk
- 20 g coriander leaves

Tom yam khung — *Spicy soup with chilli pepper, lemongrass, galangal root, coriander, mushrooms and prawns*

KHUNG

Preparation

Remove the heads from the prawns, peel and devein them.

Cook the heads and the shells in the water for 5 minutes. Sieve the broth.

Bruise the lemongrass, remove the tough outer layer and coarsely chop the stems. Brush the galangal root and coriander root or stems to clean them, then slice and bruise them. Peel the onion and slice into thin wedges. Slice the chilli pepper in half lengthways.

Add the lemongrass, galangal root, coriander root, onion, red chilli peppers and lime leaves to the broth. Add the *nam prik pao* and bring to a boil, stirring, until the chilli paste has dissolved. Cook the prawns briefly in the broth.

Clean the shimeji mushrooms and add them to the broth. Add the sugar. Season the tom yam to taste with fish sauce and stop stirring. Remove from the heat. Add the lime juice and condensed milk. Season further to taste if desired.

Garnish with coriander.

Ingredients

Serves 2 to 3 people

- 2 kg mussels
- 2 small red (Thai) chilli peppers
- 1 clove garlic
- 3 stalks lemongrass
- 1 galangal root
- a handful coriander stems and leaves, preferably with the roots
- 4 lime leaves
- a few sprigs Thai basil

Preparation

Rinse the mussels a couple of times in running water. Slice the chilli pepper in half lengthways and bruise them slightly. Bruise and peel the garlic. Bruise the lemongrass. Slice the galangal root.

Pour half a litre of water in a pan. Add the chilli peppers, garlic, lemongrass, galangal root, coriander and lime leaves. Bring to a boil and add the mussels.

Cover the pan with a lid and shake the pan a few times. The mussels are cooked when the shells are open.

Serve the mussels with *nam jim seafood* (page 205) and garnish with Thai basil.

Hoi maleng phoe — *Thai-style mussels*

MALENG
PHOE

Kanom jeen namya — *Thai spaghetti with whitefish*

This simple curry with whitefish is very popular in Thailand. Serve with *khanom jeen*, or Thai spaghetti.

Ingredients

Serves 2 people

200 to 250 g *khanom jeen* (fermented rice noodles)

For the fish:
· 1 stalk lemongrass
· 1 to 2 g *krachai* (fingerroot - Asian supermarket)
· 200 ml water
· 5 slices galangal root
· 300 g dorado or sea bass fillet

For the curry sauce:
· 12 to 15 dried chilli peppers
· 1 stalk lemongrass
· 5 slices galangal root
· 3 tablespoons chopped *krachai*
· 5 cloves garlic
· ⅓ cup finely chopped shallots
· 1 teaspoon turmeric powder
· 1 teaspoon *gapi* (fermented shrimp paste)
· 1½ cups coconut milk
· 1 to 2 tablespoons palm sugar
· 2 to 3 tablespoons fish sauce
· 1 to 2 tablespoons tamarind juice

For the accompanying ingredients:
· 50 g long beans
· 50 g bean sprouts
· 50 g Thai basil

Preparation

Remove the tough outer layer from the lemongrass and slice the bottom into slices. Coarsely chop the *krachai*. Bring the water to a boil and add the lemon juice, galangal root and *krachai*. Poach the fish in the broth until cooked and set briefly aside.

Soak the dried peppers in warm water until softened. Remove the tough outer layer from the lemongrass and slice the bottom into slices. Combine the soaked peppers, lemongrass, galangal root, *krachai*, peeled garlic, peeled and chopped shallots, turmeric powder, shrimp paste, coconut milk, palm sugar, fish sauce and tamarind juice in a blender. Blend until smooth.

Heat the curry over low heat. Flatten the fish and stir it into the curry.

Cook the *khanom jeen* according to the instructions on the packet. Soak immediately in a bowl of cold water. Take a handful of spaghetti and twirl them to form nests. Drain on a paper towel.

Serve the *khanom jeen* with the fish curry. Place the accompanying ingredients next to the dish.

KOON: 'Shrimp paste (*ga-pi*) and fermented fish sauce (*naam plaa*) are used in the Thai kitchen as salty seasonings. In the coastal regions, shrimp are used to make *ga-pi* but we didn't have that where I lived. Instead, we used small fish that were trapped as by-catch in the nets that were used to fish in the river. The fermented fish paste is called *plaa ra*. Grandma kept her *plaa ra* outside in earthenware pots and knew simply by smelling it when the paste was ripe enough to use.

‘*Gai-pi* and *plaa ra* have a very intense flavour and taste; you shouldn’t use too much of it. It gives Thai dishes that typical Boo Raan flavour.

Preferably use Thai shrimp paste. You can find this in Asian supermarkets, and it keeps quite long in a tightly sealed container.’

TOD MAN KHUNG

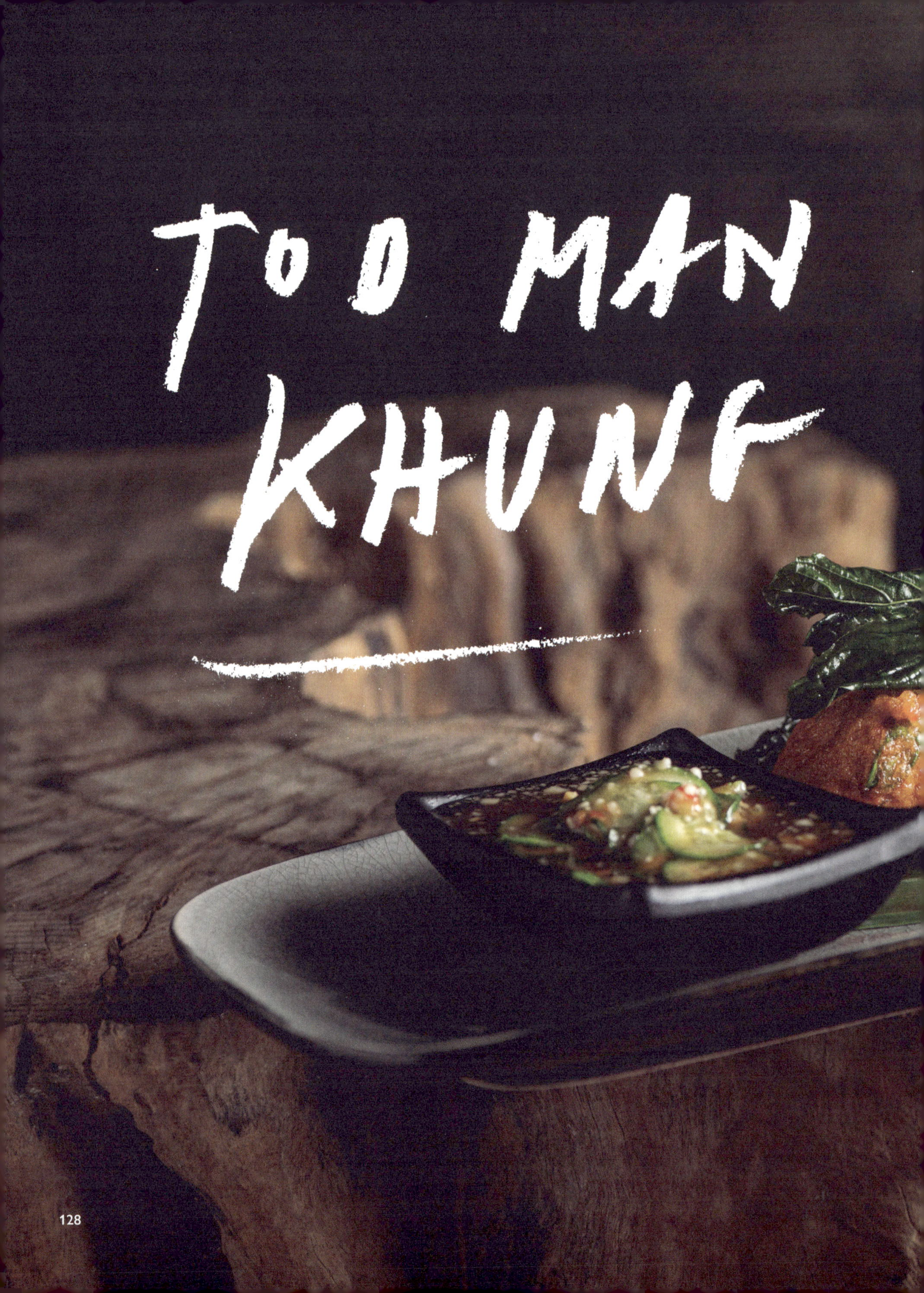

Ingredients

Makes 12 to 15 cakes

- 350 g peeled prawns (16/18 count)
- 1 egg
- 1 tablespoon red curry paste (page 51)
- ½ teaspoon sugar
- 1 tablespoon flour
- 8 lime leaves
- 3 long beans, finely chopped
- (sunflower) oil for frying
- a couple of fresh *krapow* (Thai basil) leaves

Preparation

Devein the prawns. Combine the prawns with the egg, curry paste, sugar and flour in the blender until smooth.

Remove the central vein from the lime leaves and slice them julienne into thin matchsticks. Add them to the prawn paste together with the chopped long beans. Stir everything together well. Let the paste set covered in the fridge for an hour.

With moist hands, knead balls weighing 30 to 35 grams each from the prawn mixture. Flatten them slightly and deep-fry them in oil at about 170 °C.

Serve the shrimp cakes with a sweet and sour chilli dipping sauce (*sod priawan*, page 206), cucumber dressing (page 204) and a couple of deep-fried *krapow* leaves.

Tod man khung — *Prawn cakes*

KHUNG PAW

The secret to *khung paw* lies in the marinade and the way the prawns are grilled. They taste best when you grill them over charcoal, but you can also use a grill pan.

Ingredients

Serves 2 to 3 people

- 4 to 6 black tiger prawns (4/6 count)
- 3 cloves garlic
- 20 black peppercorns
- 4 tablespoons oyster sauce
- 2 tablespoons soy sauce

Preparation

Slice the prawns open down the belly, but don't slice all the way through so you can flatten them out. Devein.

Grind the peeled garlic and peppercorns down to a fine paste with a mortar and pestle. Combine the mixture with the oyster sauce and soy sauce. Place the prawns in the marinade, cover and set aside to rest.

Grill the prawns over hot charcoal on the shell side until the meat starts to turn white and glisten. Turn them over and cook for an additional 30 seconds if needed and serve immediately with *nam jim seafood* (page 205).

Serve with jasmine rice.

YAM WOONGSEN THALEE

Ingredients

Serves 2 to 3 people

· 150 g squid
· 150 g peeled prawns (16/18 count)
· 8 to 10 white beech mushrooms (white shemeji)
· 200 g cellophane noodles
· 1 onion
· ½ carrot
· 1 red bird's eye chilli pepper
· 1 green bird's eye chilli pepper
· 12 cherry tomatoes
· handful coriander
· handful mint leaves
· 70 g celery (only the thin young stalks)
· 2 spring onions

For the dressing:
· 5 tablespoons lime juice
· 3 tablespoons fish sauce
· 1 tablespoon sugar
· ½ teaspoon chilli paste (*nam prik pao*)
· 1 clove of garlic

For the accompaniments:
· salad
· sprigs of coriander

Preparation

Slice the squid into 2-cm rings and blanch 2 to 3 minutes in boiling water. Peel and devein the prawns. Then clean the beech mushrooms. Blanch the prawns and the beech mushrooms 1 to 2 minutes in boiling water. Pour off the water and allow to cool. Prepare the cellophane noodles according to the instructions on the packaging.

For the dressing, combine the lime juice with the fish sauce and sugar. Keep stirring until the sugar has dissolved. Add the chilli paste. Peel and snipper the garlic. Stir the garlic into the dressing.

Peel the onion and slice into rings. Slice the carrot into thin strips (julienne). Slice the bird's eye chilli peppers in rings and halve the cherry tomatoes. Finely chop the coriander and the mint. Slice the celery into 2-centimetre pieces. Finely chop the spring onions.

Combine the prawns, squid, beech mushrooms, onion, carrot, peppers, tomatoes, coriander, mint, celery and spring onion in a large bowl. Add the cellophane noodles and dressing and toss carefully to coat everything well.

Serve the salad with lettuce or cellophane noodles and a couple of coriander sprigs.

Pla nung see ieuw

Ingredients

Serves 2 people

Ingredients:
· 50 g fresh ginger
· 30 g white onion
· 30 g shiitake mushrooms
· ¼ pointed sweet pepper
· 2 young, thin stalks celery
· 1 clove garlic
· 300 g cod fillet, with skin
· 2 tablespoons soy sauce
· 1 tablespoon sesame oil
· pepper

For the sauce:
· 6 tablespoons soy sauce
· 4 tablespoons oyster sauce
· 2 tablespoons sesame oil
· 4 tablespoons fish stock
· pepper

Preparation

Peel the ginger and slice into thin matchsticks. Peel the onion and slice into thin rings. Chop the shiitake mushrooms into pieces and the pointed sweet pepper into thin strips (julienne). Finely chop the celery.

For the sauce, combine the soy sauce with the oyster sauce, sesame oil and fish stock. Season with pepper.

Finely chop the garlic and put in a bowl. Place the fish on top of the garlic and spoon the sauce over the top. Divide the vegetables over the fish. Place the bowl in a steamer basket and cover with a lid. Steam the fish until tender, about 10 to 12 minutes.

Tip →

You can also prepare the fish in a steamer oven or wrap the fish in parchment paper (*en papilotte*) and bake the fish for 15 minutes in the oven at 180 °C.

SHOE SHEE

Ingredients
Serves 1 to 2 people

- 4 tablespoons sunflower oil
- 1 tablespoon red curry paste (page 51)
- 150 ml creamy coconut milk
- 2 teaspoons fish sauce
- 1 teaspoon palm sugar
- 3 tablespoons fish stock
- 2 lime leaves
- ¼ pointed sweet pepper
- 200 g cod fillet
- sunflower oil
- pepper

Preparation

Heat the sunflower oil and fry the curry paste until it starts to become fragrant. Add the coconut milk, fish sauce, palm sugar and fish stock. Bring to a boil and lower the heat.

Slice the lime leaves and pointed sweet pepper into thin strips (julienne). Add them to the sauce.

Fry the fish in a splash of sunflower oil and season with freshly ground pepper. Pat the fish dry with paper towels, place it on a plate and spoon the curry sauce over the top.

TIP → You can experiment with the curry paste and coconut milk amounts. The less curry paste you use, the milder the flavour. Too much coconut milk can make the sauce too runny, so use creamy coconut milk for this dish.

PLA

Although Thai cuisine doesn't really work with first and main courses, we consider this dorado dish to be a starter.

PLA TOD YAM TAKRAY

Ingredients

Serves 2 to 3 people

For the dressing:
· 4 tablespoons lime juice
· 1 tablespoon palm sugar
· 2 tablespoons fish sauce
· 1 small (Thai) chilli pepper

For the dorado:
· 5 stalks lemongrass
· 60 g cashews
· oil for frying
· 350 g dorado fillet
· 1 (Thai) shallot
· fresh mint leaves

Preparation

First, make the dressing. Combine the lime juice with the fish sauce and sugar. Very finely chop the chilli pepper and stir it into the mixture.

Use only the bottom 10 centimetres of the lemongrass stalk. Remove the tough outer layer and very finely chop the stems. Deep-fry the cashews until they're golden brown and leave them to drain on paper towels.

Dice the fish into 3 x 3-centimetre cubes. Deep-fry the fish until crispy and drain on paper towels.

Finely chop the nuts. Finely chop the peeled shallot. Stir the nuts, lemongrass and shallot into the dressing. Spoon the dressing over the fried fish and garnish with fresh mint leaves.

Mieung pla paw — *Crusted sea bass*

Ingredients

Serves 2 to 3 people

· 3 tablespoons tapioca flour
· 3 tablespoons water
· pepper
· salt
· 2 stalks lemongrass
· 30 g fresh ginger
· 5 lime leaves
· 500 g whole sea bass (gutted and scaled)
· 30 g fresh coriander
· 4 tablespoons sunflower oil

For the garnish:
· 15 crispy iceberg lettuce leaves
· 15 mint leaves
· 15 Thai basil leaves
· 30 g coriander leaves

For the dressing:
· *Nam jim seafood* (page 205)

Preparation

Mix the flour with the water to make a smooth paste. Season with salt and pepper.

Chop the lemongrass into pieces. Peel the ginger and chop into pieces. Finely shred the lime leaves. Fill the fish's belly with the lemongrass, ginger, lime leaves and coriander.

Coat the fish on both sides with the flour paste. Fry the sea bass in a grill pan in a little sunflower oil or on the barbecue. Carefully remove the fish from the crust.

Use the lettuce leaves like a taco shell and fill them with pieces of fish and the remaining ingredients. Garnish with a spoonful of dressing.

Serve with *khanom jeen* (Thai spaghetti).

Serve this sea bass wrapped in a crispy iceberg lettuce leaf, like a taco.

VEGETABLE dishes

Ingredients
Serves 4 people

· 100 g cellophane noodles
· 80 g unripe mango (or sour green apple if you can't find unripe mango)
· 60 g carrots
· 4 sheets rice paper
· 50 g mint leaves
· 50 g coriander leaves
· 4 leaves crispy lettuce, such as iceberg lettuce

Preparation

Soak the cellophane noodles as indicated on the packet. Slice the mango and carrots into thin strips (julienne).

Soak the rice paper 15 seconds in lukewarm water. Place the rice paper sheets on a chopping board.

Place the ingredients on the sheet in the following order: lettuce leaf, cellophane noodles, mango strips, carrot strips, a couple of mint leaves and a couple of coriander leaves.

Move all the ingredients to the bottom of the rice sheet and roll from the bottom up. Fold the sides in halfway and continue to roll. Slice the roll diagonally and serve with *nam jim seafood* (page 205) or sesame dressing (page 205).

POPIA SOD

KOON: 'Thai mangoes are the tastiest, but are also often the most expensive. We only use ripe mangoes at Boo Raan for desserts when they're in season and very sweet. My grandma used to make sweets from ripe mangoes. She cooked the flesh to a pulp and then spread it out on a banana leaf before leaving it to dry in the sun. Once the moisture had evaporated, you were left with a sticky layer, which my grandma then rolled up into sweets. In Thailand, ripe mango with sticky rice is a popular snack.

‘We use unripe mangoes for salads. Their flavour is fresher and more sour, a perfect match all sorts of savoury dishes. In Thailand, you can also buy unripe mangoes with a spicy dipping sauce at every market.’

KAW POTH TOD

This is a wonderful vegetarian street-food snack.

Ingredients

Makes 6 to 8 cakes

- 3 tablespoons tempura flour
- 1 tablespoon tapioca flour
- 1 egg
- 3 tablespoons water
- pepper
- salt
- 120 g tinned sweetcorn (or the kernels from 2 corn cobs)
- oil for deep-frying

Preparation

Combine the tempura flour with the tapioca flour, egg and water, but make sure the paste isn't too thick. Season with salt and pepper. Stir the corn kernels into the mixture.

Heat the oil in a large pan or deep fryer. Take a large tablespoon of the mixture and carefully let it slide into the hot oil. Don't fry too many cakes at once. Drain on a kitchen towel.

Serve the cakes with *sod priawan* (page 206) or another sweet and sour dip.

TIP → Add a spoonful of *nam prik pao* chilli paste to the corn mixture for a bit of extra spice.

IN THE
WOK

PHAD KRAPAW

Ingredients

Serves 2 people

- 300 g chicken breast
- 1 clove garlic
- 1 to 2 small (Thai) chilli peppers
- ½ onion
- 60 g long beans
- 3 tablespoons sunflower oil + extra
- 2 tablespoons oyster sauce
- 2 tablespoons soy sauce
- 60 g holy basil
- 2 eggs
- pepper

Preparation

Slice the chicken into thin strips or finely chop the chicken. Peel the garlic and chop the chilli peppers into pieces. Grind them to a coarse paste using a mortar and pestle. Peel the onion and slice into thin wedges. Coarsely chop the long beans.

Heat a splash of olive oil in a wok over a high heat. Fry the chilli and the garlic in the hot oil. After 20 seconds, add the chicken and continue to stir so the garlic doesn't burn and the chicken remains white. Add the onion and long beans. After a minute and a half, add the oyster sauce and the soy sauce. Keep stirring.

Stir the basil through the chicken and serve in deep plates. Serve with a fried egg and rice if desired.

Thai-style fried eggs are fried in oil. Heat 3 table-spoons oil in a pan and fry the eggs until they are brown and crispy at the edges. Season with pepper.

Phad krapaw — *Stir-fried chicken with or without fried egg*

Pad kra pao is a spicy stir-fried dish with the subtle flavour of holy basil. Unlike the basil used in the West, its leaves are serrated and have small hairs on them. This basil tastes a bit spicier with just a hint of nutmeg or cloves.

This chicken is often eaten for lunch. It is a typical street food dish that you can find at countless stalls, where this dish is made fresh while you wait. You can eat it with rice, but it is particularly popular with a fried egg. Then the dish is called *kao pad kra pao kai dao,* which loosely translates to rice with stir-fried chicken, holy basil and fried egg. A Thai egg is fried in plenty of oil so the egg white turns crispy brown at the edges.

Don't feel like chicken? Try it with pork, beef or seafood.
The vegetarian version is made using tofu or mushrooms.

Krapaw Thalee — *Seafood with Holy Basil*

PHAD THAI

This is probably the most famous Thai dish in the world.

Ingredients

Serves 1 to 2 people

- 150 g noodles
- 1 shallot
- 50 g tofu
- 30 g *kow choi* (Chinese chives) or young leek
- 6 to 8 prawns
- 3 tablespoons sunflower oil
- 1 egg
- 4 tablespoons soy sauce
- 1 tablespoon cane sugar
- 2 tablespoons tamarind juice
- 30 g bean sprouts
- 1 tablespoons unsalted peanuts
- roasted chilli powder (page 211)
- ¼ lime

Preparation

Soak the noodles in cold water. Drain in a colander.

Slice the peeled shallot into thin rings and dice the tofu. Slice the *kow chi*, young leek into thin, 4-centimetre strips. Remove the head, shell and vein from the prawns.

Heat the oil in a wok and sauté the shallots. Add the tofu. Fry the prawns with the tofu. Add the noodles and briefly stir-fry everything.

Move everything over to the side and crack the egg into the wok. Stir the egg into the other ingredients. Add the soy sauce, sugar and tamarind juice and fry for a little longer.

Add the bean sprouts and the *kow choi* strips to the wok and stir-fry briefly. Dry-roast the peanuts in a non-stick pan without any fat. Crush them fine with a mortar and pestle. Garnish the *phad thai khung* with the peanuts and roasted chilli powder (page 211). Serve with a lime wedge.

KHUNG

PHAD THAI KAI HOA

Instead of adding egg to the *phad thai*, you can also serve the *phad thai* in an omelette. This is how *phad thai* is eaten at food stalls in Thailand.

Lightly beat 2 eggs and make a thin omelette using plenty of sunflower oil. Spoon the *phad thai* onto half the omelette and fold the omelette over to close.

Phad thai kai hoa — *Egg-wrapped fried noodles*

Koon: 'Where I come from, we use duck eggs instead of chicken eggs for our omelettes. They're slightly larger, which means you can feed more people with them. To season the omelette, we use a little fish sauce and some finely chopped spring onion or garlic. We then fry the omelette in plenty of oil or lard. The omelettes are not supposed to be deep-fried, but they should be nice and crispy at the edges. We usually serve them alongside rice to make a meal. Thais also eat soft-boiled eggs, but instead of dipping toast into the eggs, they use balls of sticky rice.'

PHAD PAK

The secret to stir-frying is in the high temperature. The vegetables should be stir-fried as quickly as possible so they remain crunchy. If you stir-fry over low heat, the vegetables will 'steam' rather than fry and lose their crunch.

Ingredients

Serves 1 to 2 people

- 1 carrot
- 1 pak choi
- 4 spears green asparagus
- ½ white onion
- 4 broccoli florets or a couple of Bimi florets
- 1 small (Thai) chilli pepper
- 1 clove garlic
- 4 tablespoons sunflower oil
- 16 sugar snaps or mangetouts
- 12 shimeji mushrooms
- 1 tablespoon soy sauce
- 2 tablespoons oyster sauce
- pepper
- 1 teaspoon sugar

Preparation

Peel the carrot and slice into diagonal slices 3 centimetres thick. Slice the pak choi into long strips, the asparagus into 3-centimetre pieces and the peeled onion into thin wedges. Thinly slice the broccoli. You can leave the Bimi whole. Crush the chilli pepper and garlic using a mortar and pestle.

Heat the oil in a wok and sauté the garlic and chilli. Turn up the heat as high as you can and then first stir-fry the carrot, followed by the pak choi. Add the onion, asparagus and broccoli. Finally, add the sugar snaps and the shimeji mushrooms and season with soy sauce, oyster sauce, salt and pepper.

Remove the vegetables from the heat while they're still crunchy and serve immediately.

KAI PHAD MED MA MUANG

Ingredients

Serves 2 people

- 300 g chicken, drumsticks, thigh meat or fillet
- 1 tablespoon soy sauce
- 100 g tempura flour
- 75 g cashews
- 4 tablespoons sunflower oil
- 3 cloves garlic
- 1 onion
- 1 to 2 red (Thai) chilli peppers
- ½ pointed sweet pepper
- 2 tablespoons oyster sauce
- 1 teaspoon sugar
- 1 spring onion
- a few dried chilli peppers

Preparation

Slice the chicken into thin strips. Combine with the soy sauce and set aside to marinate.
Divide the flour between two bowls. Add a splash of water to one bowl and stir to a smooth paste. Coat the chicken strips first with the dry flour and then with the flour paste. Set aside.
Roast the cashews in 1 tablespoon oil and pat them dry with a paper towel.
Crush the garlic and slice the peeled onion into wedges.
Finely grind the chilli peppers with a mortar and pestle. Heat the rest of the oil in a wok and sauté the garlic with the onion and chilli peppers. Add the chicken and fry until golden brown.
Slice the pointed sweet pepper into thin strips. Add the pointed sweet pepper, oyster sauce and sugar to the chicken and stir-fry. Add a splash of water if the dish becomes too dry.
Slice the spring onion into not too small rings. Remove the wok from heat and add the spring onions and cashews.
Garnish with some fried dried chilli peppers and serve with jasmine rice.

KAI PHAD KHING

Ingredients

Serves 1 to 2 people

- 250 g chicken breast
- 8 cm fresh ginger
- 1 clove garlic
- 1 to 2 small (Thai) chilli peppers
- 4 tablespoons sunflower oil
- black pepper
- 2 tablespoons soy sauce
- 3 tablespoons oyster sauce
- 1 teaspoon sugar
- 12 thin strips pointed sweet pepper
- 1 spring onion, coarsely chopped

Preparation

Slice the chicken into thin strips. Peel the ginger and slice into thin matchsticks.

Grind the chilli pepper and garlic down to a coarse paste using a mortar and pestle. Sauté it in a splash of oil in the wok. Add half the ginger and stir-fry for a minute.

Add the chicken and season with pepper. Stir in the soy sauce, oyster sauce and sugar.

Add the remaining ginger, pointed sweet pepper and spring onion as soon as the chicken is cooked. Stir-fry one more minute.

Serve with jasmine rice.

KHUNG KRATIAM

Ingredients

Serves 2 people

- 12 prawns (13/15 count)
- 100 g coriander
- 5 coriander roots or 20 coriander stems
- 6 cloves garlic
- 4 tablespoons oyster sauce
- 2 tablespoons soy sauce
- 1 teaspoon palm sugar
- 4 tablespoons sunflower oil
- white pepper

Preparation

Remove the head, shell and vein from the shrimp.

Combine the coriander, coriander root or stems, and peeled garlic in a mortar and crush them to a coarse paste. Mix with the oyster sauce, soy sauce and sugar. Season with pepper. Marinate the prawns for 15 minutes in this mixture.

Heat the oil in a wok. Remove the prawns from the marinade and fry them over a high heat. Drain on paper towels.

Add the marinade to the wok and heat until the garlic starts to turn golden brown. Add a small splash of water to deglaze the pan if you wish. Serve the prawns with the garlic sauce.

TIP → You can also use pork or chicken instead of prawns.

NO MAÍ VARANG KLUNG

This is a wonderful dish for a sharing menu. You can also make a vegetarian version by replacing the prawns with tofu.

Ingredients

Serves 2 people

- 6 to 8 prawns
- 200 g green asparagus
- 1 clove garlic
- 3 bird's eye chilli peppers or 1 red chilli pepper
- 4 tablespoons sunflower oil
- black pepper
- 2 tablespoons oyster sauce
- 2 tablespoons soy sauce
- 2 tablespoons vegetable stock or water

Preparation

Peel and devein the prawns. Peel the asparagus and slice them diagonally into 4-centimetre pieces.

Crush the peeled garlic and chilli peppers with a mortar and pestle to a fine paste.

Heat a splash of sunflower oil in the wok. Add the garlic and chilli and fry 10 seconds. Make sure the garlic doesn't burn. Turn up the heat and stir-fry the asparagus a couple of minutes.

Move the asparagus off to the side and add the prawns to the wok. Stir-fry the prawns 30 seconds to 1 minute over a high heat. Season with pepper and add the oyster sauce and soy sauce. Add a little water or stock.

Tip Preferably stir-fry everything in one pan and keep an eye on the cooking time. You can also stir-fry the prawns and the asparagus separately (in the same oil) if you prefer. Combine everything just before serving if you do so.

NEU HORAPA

Ingredients
Serves 1 to 2 people

· 200 g steak (sirloin)
· 1 clove garlic
· 4 tablespoons sunflower oil
· black pepper
· 2 tablespoons oyster sauce
· 1 tablespoon soy sauce
· 10 strips red pointed sweet pepper
· handful Thai basil leaves

Preparation

Slice the beef into slices, 4 x 6 centimetres and half a centimetre thick.

Peel and crush the garlic. Heat the oil and fry the garlic 10 seconds. Make sure the garlic doesn't burn. Turn up the heat and sear the meat. Season with pepper, oyster sauce and soy sauce.

Add the pointed sweet pepper to the wok, toss three times and then add the Thai basil. Serve immediately.

Tip Make sure that all the ingredients are prepared and chopped beforehand and work quickly because the meat requires very little cooking time. If you cook the meat too long, it becomes leathery.

PHAD PED

Ingredients

Serves 2 people

- 200 g squid (tentacles and body)
- 1 clove garlic
- 1 small red (Thai) chilli pepper
- 30 g long beans
- 2 lime leaves
- 4 tablespoons sunflower oil
- 20 g or 2 sprigs fresh green peppercorns (Asian supermarket)
- 2 tablespoons oyster sauce
- 2 tablespoons soy sauce
- 2 twigs Thai pea aubergine
- 2 Thai aubergines, the size of a plum
- 2 tablespoons bamboo shoots
- 3 tablespoons vegetable stock or water
- 12 strips pointed sweet pepper

Preparation

Clean the squid and slice the body into rings. Crush the peeled garlic and chilli peppers to a fine paste using a mortar and pestle. Chop the long beans into pieces and the lime leaves into thin strips.

Heat a splash of oil in the wok and fry the garlic and chilli pepper for 10 seconds. Add the fresh peppercorns.

Remove the Thai pea aubergines from the twigs. Turn up the heat and add the squid to the wok. Stir-fry for about 1 to 2 minutes. Stir in the soy sauce, oyster sauce, Thai aubergines, bamboo shoots and long beans. Stir-fry for 2 more minutes and add some water or vegetable stock to deglaze if needed.

Finally, add the sweet pointed peppers and the lime leaves. Stir-fry for 30 more seconds.

Serve with jasmine rice.

Phad ped plamuk — *Squid with green chillies from the wok*

PLAMUK

RAW VEGETABLES

Thais always serve a large plate with raw, fresh vegetables and herbs with their dishes. This can include long beans cut into strips, sticks of cucumber, the hard centre of an iceberg or red leaf lettuce, and Thai basil leaves.

SIDE DISHES

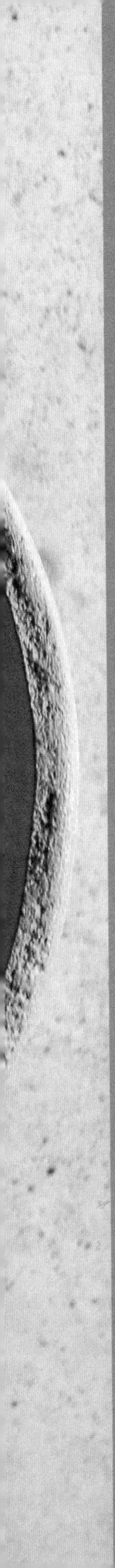

KHAW PHAD

Ingredients

Serves 2 to 3 people

· 1 carrot
· 40 g leek
· ½ onion
· 1 spring onion
· 1 clove garlic
· 3 tablespoons sunflower oil
· 2 eggs
· 400 g jasmine rice, cooked and cooled
· black pepper
· 2 tablespoons soy sauce

Preparation

Very finely dice the carrot. Slice the leek into thin slices, the peeled onion into thin wedges and the spring onion into thin rings. Finely chop and crush the peeled garlic.

Heat the oil in a wok and sauté the garlic. Add the carrot and the onion and turn up the heat slightly. Break the eggs in the wok and lightly beat them. Add the cold rice and stir with a wooden spatula. Season to taste with freshly ground black pepper and soy sauce.

Let the rice change colour slightly. Remove from the heat and stir in the spring onion rings.

This fried rice dish is still very popular with people living in the countryside. Street vendors often used to sell this on the train. They would board at different locations to provide people travelling from the north to Bangkok with a fresh meal.

KHAW PAD ROT FAI

Ingredients

Serves 2 people

- ½ white onion
- ½ cucumber
- 1 spring onion
- ½ clove garlic
- 125 g Chinese broccoli
- 1 large tomato
- 2 tablespoons sunflower oil
- 2 eggs
- 250 g jasmine rice, cooked and cooled
- black pepper
- 1 teaspoon sugar
- 2 tablespoons light soy sauce
- 1 teaspoon dark soy sauce

Preparation

Slice the peeled onion into thin slices, and the cucumber and spring onion into large pieces. Finely chop and crush the peeled garlic.

Divide the broccoli into florets and coarsely chop them. Chop the tomato into pieces.

Heat the oil in a wok and sauté the garlic. Add the broccoli and the onion and turn up the heat. Break the eggs in the wok. Lightly beat them and add the rice. Keep stirring with a wooden spatula. Add the tomato and season with black pepper, sugar and light and dark soy sauce.

Let the rice change colour slightly. Remove the wok from the heat and serve immediately with the cucumber and spring onion pieces.

SOM TAM

Ingredients

Serves 1 to 2 people

- 1 large carrot
- 150 g green (unripe) papaya
- a pinch of shrimp paste (optional, but always included in Thailand)
- 3 cloves garlic
- 2 small red (Thai) chilli peppers
- 2 tablespoons palm or cane sugar
- 2 tablespoons fish sauce
- 2 tablespoons lime juice
- 8 cherry tomatoes
- 50 g long beans (or string beans)
- 20 g unsalted peanuts

Preparation

Peel and grate the carrot and papaya. Soak them 5 minutes in iced water.

Grind the shrimp paste, peeled garlic, chilli peppers and sugar down to a fine paste using a mortar and pestle. Add the fish sauce and the lime juice and stir thoroughly.

Slice the cherry tomatoes in half and add them to the mortar. Bruise them slightly so the juice blends in with the other ingredients.

Chop the beans into 5-centimetre pieces. Dry-roast the peanuts in a non-stick pan without any fat. Add the beans and the peanuts to the rest of the ingredients and mash everything together.

Add the papaya and the carrot and stir well. The salad should be spicy. Add lime juice, sugar or fish sauce to taste. Serve immediately.

KOON: 'I love green papaya salad. As a child, I could have eaten this salad all day – as breakfast, lunch and dinner. The secret ingredient is the spoonful of shrimp or fermented fish paste that adds spice to the salad. When we started with the restaurant, I didn't dare add it because I was afraid that guests would find the paste too overpowering. Today, I do add it in, and we've been receiving nothing but praise for it. My favourite way to eat *tom sam* is with my hands, but we don't go that far at Boo Raan. Besides green papaya, unripe mangoes and pomelos are often used in all sorts of salads.

‘Sometimes raw or blanched vegetables are added, but the salad must remain crunchy. The dressing often contains four basic flavours: sour lime, sweet palm sugar, spicy chillies and salty fish sauce. You garnish the dish with roasted peanuts, cashews or chilli peppers. In Thailand, tiny dried shrimp with a fermented flavour are mixed into the *tom sam* but, sadly, they are hard to find here.’

GALAM
PLEE
PHAD
NAM
PLA

This is a very quick and simple stir-fried dish that you can eat as a side, or as a lunch served with rice.

Ingredients

Serves 4 people

- ½ pointed cabbage
- 5 cloves garlic
- ½ small (Thai) chilli pepper
- 4 tablespoons sunflower oil
- 2 tablespoons fish sauce
- white pepper

Preparation

Slice the cabbage into 5 x 5-centimetre pieces.

Peel and coarsely crush the garlic cloves with a knife. Grind the chilli peppers to a coarse paste. Sauté the garlic and chilli in the oil. Turn up the heat and add the pointed cabbage. Stir-fry for 3 minutes and add the fish sauce. Season with pepper.

Serve immediately.

PHAD MIÈ SUA

Ingredients

Serves 1 to 2 people

- 150 g Chinese wheat noodles
- 1 pak choi
- 1 carrot
- 5 shiitake mushrooms
- 50 g pointed cabbage
- ½ clove garlic
- 4 tablespoons sunflower oil
- 2 tablespoons soy sauce
- 2 tablespoons oyster sauce
- pepper
- salt
- 1 teaspoon sugar
- 2 tablespoons vegetable stock

Preparation

Soak the noodles in water for 5 minutes. Drain in a colander.

Slice the pak choi into thin strips, the carrot into thin slices and the shiitake in pieces. Chop the cabbage into 5 x 5-centimetre pieces.

Crush the peeled garlic. Heat the oil in a wok and saté the garlic. Add the carrot and cook for a couple of minutes. Then add the pointed cabbage, pak choi and shiitake mushrooms. Stir-fry for 2 minutes and then add the soaked noodles. Season to taste with soy sauce, oyster sauce, freshly ground pepper, salt and sugar. Finally, add the vegetable stock. Stir-fry for a couple of seconds over a high heat and serve immediately.

Sauces & Dressings

Cucumber Dressing

Ingredients

- juice from 2 to 3 limes
- 1 tablespoon sugar
- salt
- 3 mini cucumbers
- ½ red onion
- ¼ red pointed sweet pepper

Preparation

Heat the lime juice and dissolve the sugar in the juice. Season with a pinch of salt and let the liquid cool.

Thinly slice the cucumber and the peeled onion and dice the pointed sweet pepper into small cubes.

Combine the vegetables with the sweetened lime juice just before serving.

Peanut Sauce

Ingredients

- 1 tablespoon sunflower oil
- 3 tablespoons dry (*massaman*) curry paste (shop-bought from the supermarket)
- 200 ml coconut milk
- 120 g unsalted roasted peanuts
- 2 tablespoons tamarind juice
- 2 tablespoons palm or cane sugar
- salt

Preparation

Heat the oil in a pan and sauté the curry paste about 30 seconds. Add the coconut milk and bring to the boil, stirring all the while.

Finely chop the peanuts. Add them with the tamarind juice, sugar and a pinch of salt to the coconut milk. Cook the sauce over a low heat for about 4 minutes.

Serve the sauce with dishes like chicken satay.

SESAME SEED DRESSING

Ingredients

- 2 tablespoon sesame seeds
- 2 tablespoons mayonnaise or full-fat yoghurt
- 2 tablespoons soy sauce
- 1 tablespoon mirin
- 4 tablespoons sesame oil
- 3 tablespoons lime juice
- black pepper

Preparation

Dry-roast the sesame seeds in a non-stick pan without any fat.

Combine the mayonnaise or full-fat yoghurt with the roasted sesame seeds, soy sauce, mirin, sesame oil and lime juice. Season to taste with black pepper.

NAM JIM JEAW

This dipping sauce goes really well with all sorts of grilled dishes, such as *moo ping* or *kai yang*.

Ingredients

- 2 dried chilli peppers
- 1 shallot
- 3 tablespoons tamarind juice
- 1 teaspoon palm sugar
- 1 teaspoon toasted rice powder (page 211)
- 3 tablespoons fish sauce
- coriander leaves to garnish

Preparation

Very finely chop the chilli peppers and the peeled shallot. Combine them with the tamarind juice, palm sugar, rice powder and fish sauce. Garnish with fresh coriander leaves.

NAM JIM SEAFOOD

Ingredients

- 4 coriander roots or 12 coriander stems
- 50 g coriander
- 1 to 2 small green (Thai) chilli peppers
- 2 to 3 tablespoons palm sugar
- 1 clove garlic
- 50 ml fish sauce
- 100 ml lime juice

Preparation

Brush the coriander root or stems to clean them. Put the coriander roots or stems, coriander, chilli peppers, palm sugar and peeled garlic in a mortar. Grind everything down to a fine paste. Stir the fish sauce and lime juice into the paste.

Tip → You can also prepare this dish in a blender, but the mixture is more fragrant if you use a mortar and pestle. Mix the *nam jim seafood* in with the vegetables just before serving so everything looks and smells fresh.

You can buy sweet and sour dipping sauce and spruce it up. Heat the desired amount of sauce in a saucepan and add a few halved cherry tomatoes. Let the sauce reduce briefly and garnish with fresh coriander and a generous squeeze of lime juice.

With the recipes below, you can make your own *sod priawan*, a sweet and sour chilli sauce to serve with dishes such as spring rolls.

Sweet & Sour Chilli Sauce 1

Ingredients

- 2 red chilli peppers
- 1 clove garlic
- 40 g fresh ginger
- 100 ml vinegar
- 200 g sugar
- 1 tablespoon soy sauce
- 2 tablespoons tapioca flour
- 3 tablespoons water

Preparation

Remove the seeds and membrane from the chilli peppers and blend them in a blender. Peel the garlic and ginger. Blend them as well.

Heat the vinegar and dissolve the sugar in the liquid. Add the soy sauce. Remove the pan from the heat as soon as the liquid starts to thicken and before it caramelizes. Dissolve the tapioca flour in the water and stir it into the sauce to give it the desired thickness.

Season to taste with a pinch of salt, if desired.

Chill the sauce completely.

Sweet & Sour Chilli Sauce 2

We used to make this sweet and sour chilli sauce back home.

Ingredients

- 1 tablespoon unsalted peanuts
- 150 ml tamarind juice
- 200 g cane sugar
- 1 tablespoon soy sauce
- salt
- roasted chilli powder (page 211)

Preparation

Dry roast the peanuts in a non-stick pan without any fat. Crush them slightly in the mortar and pestle.

Bring the tamarind juice to a boil and dissolve the sugar in the liquid. Remove the pan from the heat as soon as the liquid starts to thicken and before it caramelizes. Add the soy sauce and season with salt. Chill the sauce.

Add crushed peanuts and chilli powder to taste.

Nam Jim Thua

Thai barbecue dipping sauce

A traditional Thai barbecue is served with *nam jim suki* as a dipping sauce. To make this sauce, you need fermented red tofu, which is not easy to find in most Western countries. Thankfully, you can buy this sauce ready-made in a bottle or replace it with *nam jim thua*.

Nam jim thua is prepared in exactly the same way as *nam jim seafood* (page 205), but you add unsalted roasted peanuts which are finely ground using a mortar and pestle. Add the nuts to the sauce just before serving; the nuts soak up the moisture, making the sauce visually less appetising.

NAM PRIK PLA

Anyone who has been to Thailand will be familiar with this spicy sauce. At Boo Raan, this sauce is often requested as an extra seasoning for all sorts of dishes.

Ingredients

- 2 to 3 green or red (Thai) chilli peppers
- 2 tablespoons fish sauce
- 2 tablespoons lime juice

Preparation

Finely chop the chili peppers. Combine them with the fish sauce and lime juice. Add some more lime juice if the mixture is too spicy.

TIP → You can also add some crushed garlic for added flavour.

KOON: '*Nam prik* literally means "spicy water". It's a typical Thai chilli sauce with a spicy or smoky flavour. The ideal sauce is a perfect balance of sour, hot and salty with just a hint of sweet. A little bit of fermented shrimp paste is often added to combine all the flavours.

'Thais eat this with almost every meal as a dipping sauce with raw or fried vegetables, omelettes, or grilled chicken or fish.'

FLAVOURINGS

SAAM KIEU

Marinade

This is a basic marinade for all sorts of grilled meat dishes.

Ingredients

- 12 black peppercorns
- 3 cloves garlic
- 4 coriander roots or 8 coriander stems
- 2 tablespoons oyster sauce
- 2 tablespoons soy sauce
- ½ teaspoon palm sugar

Preparation

Crush the peppercorns into coarse pieces using a mortar and pestle. Finely chop the peeled garlic and coriander roots or stems and also crush them using the mortar and pestle. Stir in the oyster sauce, soy sauce and sugar.

PRIK PON

Roasted chilli powder

Ingredients

- 200 g dried Thai chilli peppers
- 2 to 3 lime leaves (optional)

Preparation

Preheat the oven to 180 °C or heat a wok over a high heat. Bake the chilli peppers 5 to 7 minutes in the oven or roast them in the wok until they start to change colour and give off a smoky fragrance. Add the lime leaves if desired for added flavour.

Let the peppers cool. Grind them down to a powder in the blender or crush them using a mortar and pestle. You can store the chilli powder in an airtight container.

KAW KHUA

Toasted rice powder

Ingredients

- handful uncooked Thai sticky rice
- 1 lime leaf (optional)

Preparation

Roast the rice over a high heat in a non-stick pan without any fat. Roast until the rice starts to turn brown. Remove from the heat.

Coarsely grind the rice in a blender or using a mortar and pestle. The texture should still be grainy.

Add lime leaves to change the flavour.

BOO RAAN
TRADITIONAL THAI FOOD

TUK TUK
BOO RAAN

INDEX

Apple, tart 152
Asparagus, green 23, 170, 182
Aubergine, Thai 23, 51, 96, 186

Conversion table

Weights for dry ingredients

20g	¾ oz
25g	1 oz
40g	1½oz
50g	2oz
60g	2½oz
75g	3oz
100g	3½oz
125g	4oz
150g	5oz
175g	6oz
200g	7oz
250g	9oz
300g	11oz
350g	12oz
400g	14oz
500g	1lb 2oz
1kg	2¼lb

Liquid measures

METRIC	IMPERIAL	US
50 ml	2 fl oz	¼ cup
75 ml	3 fl oz	
100 ml	3½ fl oz	
120 ml	4 fl oz	½ cup
150 ml	5 fl oz	
200 ml	7 fl oz	
250 ml	8 fl oz	1 cup
400 ml	14 fl oz	
560 ml	18.94 fl oz	

Oven temperatures

°C	°F
160	325
170	338
180	350
220	425

COLOPHON

www.lannoo.com
Register on our website and we will regularly send you a newsletter with information about our latest books as well as interesting, exclusive offers.

Text and recipes
— Dokkoon Kapueak, Patrick De Langhe
Copywriting
— Hilde Smeesters
Translation
— Textcase
Photography
— Kris Jacobs, except p 4, 5, 6, 12, 25, 26, 28, 31, 188, 190 (Éleonore Van Bavel) and p 14, 17, 18, 19, 217, 218 (Tourism Authority of Thailand)
Graphic Design
— Tom Suykens
Typesetting
— Textcase

With our special thanks to the Tourism Authority of Thailand for sharing the pictures listed above and the information about the most beautiful destinations in Thailand.

If you have any comments or questions, please contact our editors: redactielifestyle@lannoo.com.

© Dokkoon Kapueak, Patrick De Langhe & Uitgeverij Lannoo nv, Tielt, 2021
D/2021/45/308 - NUR 440, 442
ISBN: 9789401479233

All rights reserved. Nothing from this edition may be reproduced, recorded in an automated database and/or published in any form or in any way, whether electronic, mechanical or in any other manner without the prior written permission of the publisher.

จำกัด (มหาชน)
www.cpfworldwide.com